occ. 50

On July 1, 1965

DATE DUE

DEC 17, 2002			

Demco

Harmony in
Western Music

Harmony in Western Music

Richard Franko Goldman

W · W · NORTON & COMPANY · INC ·

NEW YORK

Contents

Preface

It is immediately evident that one needs a good reason for undertaking still another harmony book. On the material of harmony, as it is traditionally studied, there are many excellent textbooks, and more appear each year. When all is considered, one is tempted to say that, for most of the objectives of traditional harmony study, the old standard text of Ernst Richter, published in 1853, is probably as good as any.

The situation of the student has changed, however, since Richter's day, as has the situation of musical technique and of music itself. Today one has to ask first, who studies traditional harmony, and second, for what purpose?

For some reason, generally unexplained, all music students "take" a year or more of harmony. What they learn is in many cases a mystery. The emphasis of the usual harmony course is on having the student complete a number of exercises with reasonable "correctness." *Whose* correctness is seldom defined. It is often a notion of correctness based on the style of Bach's chorales. But sometimes one wonders what is achieved.

The student today is in all probability not going to compose in the idiom of the Bach chorales or, for that matter, in any idiom based on conventional usage of the 18th or 19th centuries. In some respects, he no longer needs traditional or classical harmony *as a technique.* What he does need is an understanding of, and a feeling for, the harmonic principles that form the basis of his artistic heritage. He needs an understanding of musical syntax in the same sense that the student of English Literature needs to know his language: not in order to write like Shakespeare, but in order to read him. This ability, fruitfully developed, also enables him to read Eliot or Joyce. The analogy with our musical language is not far-fetched; much contemporary music, apparently not based on traditional harmony, still uses its syntax, and still reflects its disciplines.

In the second half of the 20th century we are very much interested in music written both before and after the so-called "common practice" period, the period of classical-romantic harmony extending roughly from Bach to the early 20th century. To some extent, because of a shift in perspective, the understanding of the common practice period has suffered, and it is not unusual to find students today who speak more glibly (if not necessarily more profoundly) about the music of Machaut or of Webern than they do about the music of Mozart or of Schubert. It is possible that we have already entered a new era of great importance in the history of music. It is possible that new principles of musical organization are evolving, and that the nature of musical thought is taking on new dimensions. But this, if true, still does not invalidate a consideration of the background on which our thought has been based until quite recently.

This is perfectly clear if one assumes, as I do, that the music of the 17th, 18th, and 19th centuries represents a *permanent* heritage —permanent, that is, as far as permanence is conceivable in art. But it is true that the present situation makes us see traditional harmony in a different light, and poses different conditions for its study. In a sense the study of traditional harmony becomes retrospective and historical; possibly, even, it becomes more a matter of esthetics than of technique. To put this in another way: it is perhaps no longer necessary for the student to go through a series of schematic exercises in a technique that is no longer creatively relevant, or that is relevant only in an indirect way. But it is most urgently necessary for him (and for the layman who listens to music as well) to understand the principles underlying the organization of pitch and time, as they served music for its "classical" centuries. For these principles are still applicable.

II

Thus, this book starts from certain opinions or prejudices—but these prejudices are derived from some thirty years of working with the problems both of learning and of teaching harmony in our age of widespread information which too often is accepted as a substitute for understanding or knowledge.

The first prejudice is of course that the conventional harmony book is aimed in the wrong direction; its end is too often the properly completed exercise rather than the understanding of principles, the nomenclature and assortment of chords rather than their meanings and syntactical functions or possibilities.

The second is that no student should begin the study of harmony who is not seriously interested in music and familiar, through hearing or performing, with a great deal of it. Preferably, no one should study harmony who does not have at least a rudimentary ability at the keyboard. Most important, no student should be permitted to study harmony who is insensitive to pitch.

Third, it seems to me fruitless for any student to think seriously (or pretend to think seriously) about musical techniques if he does not have a library of music at his disposal. It is music that must be his basic text, not a harmony book or a work book, be it this one or any other.

For these reasons, this book assumes that the student has at least a modest acquaintance with music of the 18th and 19th centuries and what it sounds like; that he can play at least very simple things at the keyboard; and that he can sing or whistle a simple tune. It is assumed that anyone using this book knows intervals, and has the basic vocabulary (or "rudiments of music") with which some texts commence. One cannot talk about harmony without this foundation. If these conditions eliminate certain classes of "beginners" (as accepted at many institutions), the elimination is, alas, intentional. Such beginners must really begin where it is necessary to begin.

At the same time, it is not suggested that this is a book for "advanced" students. It is designed for those who study harmony because they are interested in it rather than because it is "required." For the same reason, it is hoped that the book may be of use to general students who are not music majors, but who have sufficient interest and background in listening to music to enable them to follow it. (These students, one learns in years of teaching, are often more "musical" in many ways than those music "majors" whose interests are limited to the acquisition of mechanical skills.)

III

The basic materials of a harmony book cannot vary greatly, and I should not wish to suggest that I have discovered truths unknown to previous writers or theorists. I differ (at times quite radically) from many commonly accepted theoretical positions or deductions, especially those concerning the arbitrary quality of our conventions, the nature and function of the II and IV chords, the character and derivation of the augmented sixths, the variability of major and minor triads, and the importance of time, and of temporal ambiguities, as determining factors in hearing. (It should be observed that I say *hearing* rather than *analysis*; although no one will deny that analysis from visible data is helpful to hearing, it is what one hears, rather than what one sees—or what one can prove in theory to be operative—that makes the sense of harmonic progression.) But I have of course drawn on the experience and the wisdom of many previous writers for whom no musician can fail to have respect and admiration: Schoenberg, Schenker, Hindemith, and Piston, among others, and one should not forget old Ernst Richter or Riemann or Jadassohn. But most of all, I have drawn on Sir Donald Tovey. I have the impression that if Tovey had ever systematized his thinking about harmony, and made into a single book all of his writing bearing on the art, science, and history of traditional harmonic practice, I should not have felt it necessary or profitable to undertake this book. Tovey's ideas, more than those of any other historian or theorist, seem to me to be direct, clear, pointed, and accurate, and in demonstrable correspondence with both practice and style. It should be remarked also that Tovey wrote English that could be understood.

One further point: I have attempted to keep this book brief and clear. No book can attempt to be a complete exposition and illustration of the harmonic practices of the composers who make the history of Western music. Only general principles can be argued, and it is hoped that the examples in the Appendix are sufficient to the argument. As a teacher, even more than as an author, I insist again that the student using *any* book must be able to go to the shelves and take down musical works for perusal. Without this, there is no study of music—not even any study of an aspect of music: harmony, counterpoint, or form, arbitrary as these customary divisions are. A proper study of harmony includes considerations of the contrapuntal and the formal, as well as of matters of history and of style. It is the intention of this book to keep these considerations constantly in view.

Perhaps the greatest good a textbook or a study can do is to compel the student or reader to go to the sources that are its only justification for existence. A harmony book should make the student look at works by Bach or Mozart (or Schubert or Chopin) carefully, and with a certain end in view. Even if this end is to understand music in a certain *directed* way, something of value will have been accomplished, for this end then becomes a means to a further end: a way of understanding music in personal terms, eventually to be reflected in refinement of perception and perhaps even of performance. For we should not study harmony, or counterpoint, or form, as an end; we should not study theory: we should study music. We should not know "harmony"; we should know the music of the composers who created it.

Introduction

A harmony may be defined as the sound produced by the coincidence of several musical notes, and the science or art of harmony, as understood in Western music, may be defined as the ordering or syntax of such sounds heard successively.

The first definition involves us in a qualitative or analytical distinction, that of the concept of "harmony" as opposed to discord; it involves categorizing the kinds of sound produced by varying combinations of notes heard simultaneously. Western music in its traditional period accepts certain note combinations as consonant and useful, and defines others as dissonant and useful with special —and changing—restrictions.

The second definition involves the relation of harmonic sounds (whether consonant or dissonant) one to another, and their deployment in a continuum of time.

We are thus faced at the very outset with two primary auditory and psychological factors: *sound* and *time*. The most obvious fact about music itself is that its structure and meaning depend on the inseparable bond and relation established between these two. Even the simplest succession of single notes, which we call a melody, is evidence of this. But the highest development of Western music involves more than the succession of single notes; it is either a combination of melodies, progressing simultaneously, or a succession of harmonic sounds in which one or more melodies may or may not be of importance. In practice there is no clear separation between these two possibilities, although for several centuries the techniques of these possibilities have been separated pedagogically into the study of counterpoint and the study of harmony. Music itself does not know this separation.

Harmony, as much as melody or counterpoint, involves motion in time. Motion, in turn, involves speed, duration, and relation. Using the image of the written or printed page of music, we may say that harmony (simultaneous sound) may be read vertically and statically. But this is merely the primary element of harmony: the isolated chord, which is a *sound*, but which in itself has little or no meaning. We might, similarly, isolate any single note of a melody and identify it as C, F♯, or A♭, but such an identification would tell us nothing about the melody. Or we might take a single word of a sentence, and identify it as an adjective, perhaps denoting color or shape or size; but we could not from this deduce the meaning of the sentence, or even the nature of the noun that is modified.

The simplest element in music is a note of fixed pitch; but this element is not only the given note—*it is also its duration*, or extension in time. The note is not a fully meaningful element unless we know its absolute length, which is measurable. Thus, a whole note at $\quarternote = \text{MM}60$ lasts exactly four seconds. Its relative length, or proportion, is twice that of the half note at the same speed, or four times that of the quarter note. Manuals dealing with the rudiments of music have always made clear such relative values of notes, but few have stressed what is equally important: the measurable length of the unit itself. Music depends on one as much as on the other.

There are other considerations in connection with the single note: its intensity, quality, and (for want of a more technical term) its movement. A single note, lasting for a measurable time, may grow louder and softer (although not on some instruments, such as a piano). It may be of extreme high pitch or extreme low pitch, or may occupy that middle ground that seems most agreeable to the human ear. It may be produced by the voice or on any of a variety of instruments, having intrinsically agreeable or disagreeable timbres. All of these variables are part of music. They should not be discounted, as they usually are, even at the beginning stages of study.

Like the single note, the single harmonic unit, or chord, exists not only as a combination of pitches simultaneously heard, but also as a unit of sound heard in time. Our Western music takes a three-note complex, or *triad*, as its fundamental harmonic unit. The triad is built on ascending intervals of major or minor thirds from the lowest note, or root. Such a combination of notes (triad, chord, or harmonic unit) is subject to the same variable factors as the single note. In addition, it has its own kind of mass or density, depending on how it is deployed, or on the way its component elements may be duplicated or re-duplicated. Like the single word, or the single note, it is meaningful only in relation to other sounds. A harmonic sound, existing therefore as sound and as motion, also exists as *function* the moment it is heard in relation to another harmonic sound. Its function is understood in terms of what precedes and what follows it, and in terms of the absolute and relative times in which such movement or sequence takes place.

The analogy with language is useful, for language too is a connection in time of sounds with acquired (rather than inherent) meanings. Syntax is concerned with position and inflection, order and logic and relation; there is a syntax of music as there is of language, for the same factors are involved. Style, which is as much involved in music as in language, need not affect syntax (as it must, however, be affected by it); and if the language of Sir Thomas Browne, or of Coleridge, is stylistically very different from that of Hemingway, or of *McGuffey's Reader*, the functions of verb, adverb, or noun remain essentially the same in both. Similarly, the style of Bach differs clearly from that of Schubert or Wagner, but here again the syntactical principles on which style has evolved remain fundamentally the same in all cases.

The fundamental syntax of Western music in its traditional period is that of the harmonic language that reached its highest expressiveness from the time of Bach to the time of Wagner and Brahms. This language represents one of the greatest intellectual accomplishments of Western man. In the words of Sir Donald Tovey: "Our Western art of music stands in the unique position that its language has been wholly created by art. . . . When we trace the slow and difficult evolution of our harmonic system, we cease to wonder that it was not evolved sooner and elsewhere, and we learn to revere the miracle that it was evolved at all." *

One of the central facts about our harmonic system or language is, as Tovey points out, that it is invented. Although certain basic elements are taken from the natural overtone series, the developed relationships that form the language are, in a sense, arbitrary. The basic or fundamental tonal relationship, that of dominant and tonic, on which all further development rests, corresponds to no acoustical law, and has no "scientific" basis. † The musical relationship is wholly invented, or "created by art."

To quote Tovey again: "It is already a mature musical art that selects the acoustic facts." These facts are simple enough. Man learned very early that notes produced on a string or pipe produce a series of harmonics or overtones, as follows:

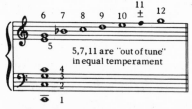

5,7,11 are "out of tune" in equal temperament

* At this point it is urgently recommended that the student or reader see, in its entirety, Tovey's essay on "Music," written originally for *The Encyclopedia Britannica*, and now included in the volume *The Forms of Music* (Meridian Books, M 36). The essay on "Harmony," in the same volume, is also indispensable.

† Some theorists—e.g. Schenker—claim that the dominant (the 3rd overtone) is the most powerful overtone, and that the dominant-tonic relationship is consequently based on an acoustical fact.

The Greeks were able to calculate mathematical ratios of vibration, or rate of vibration, and discovered a pleasingly regular order as a framework for musical speculation and esthetics. Thus, intervals having simple correspondences (as the octave, 1 to 2, or the fifth, 2 to 3) became the fundamental data of musical organization.

It is customary to relate the developed Western harmonic system to the overtone series, and up to a point this relation is in accord with the facts. But it leaves unexplained the *selection* made by art from arithmetical or acoustical data. The minor triad, for example, which is incontrovertibly of some importance in Western music, is not an obvious derivation from the overtone series. On the other hand, the interval of the fourth, which occurs early and unavoidably in the series, and which has, moreover, a simple mathematical ratio (3 to 4), has at times been defined as a consonance, and at others as a dissonance. This is the domain of art, not of physics; and this is part of what Tovey means when he states that art selects the acoustical facts.

There are further selections to be considered. The octave and the fifth have since time immemorial been established as firmly fixed points in the process of organizing sound into music. But the division of pitches within the octave is selective and variable. We take for granted our diatonic scale of seven notes, or our chromatic scale of twelve; but this is not natural law. It is possible, within the octave, to use a five-note scale (pentatonic) or a 43-note scale (as devised by Harry Partch). Almost any arithmetical or proportional division might be used as a basis for creating a usable scale within the octave; the practical limitation is simply the size of the smallest interval that the human ear can comfortably distinguish, and this is to some extent a matter of convention and of training. Our harmonic system starts from our own accepted twelve-note division, as stabilized through the adoption of equal temperament, itself a brilliant invention or achievement of art. It is a modification, for purposes of art, of the acoustical data of the overtone series.

Equal temperament orders our selective pitch system so that the intervals of any octave are identical with those of any other octave. Thus the octave C–c contains the same intervals as the octave G–g or E–e, and the major triad C–E–G has the same quality of sound (although lower or higher in pitch) as the major triad E–G♯–B or F–A–C. This means that the harmonic system developed on this basis may transpose materials from one pitch level to another, without changing the relations of parts one to another. This is a central fact in our harmonic tradition, and it is unique to Western music. It makes possible the concept of *key* or *tonality*, which is central to our harmonic scheme.

The notion of key depends primarily on the establishment of a given note as a point of rest, or as a static center about which other notes gravitate. The given note will normally serve as a point of departure and as a point of terminus. Other notes function in ordered relation to it. Such a note is known as the *tonic*, and the triad based on it is known as the *tonic triad*, the point of beginning and of ending in any conventional harmonic progression.

The traditional concept of key or tonality depends on a sense of stability and of unity. A musical composition, to be *in* a key (as we say that a certain composition is in F major) must begin and end in that key, and must center around that key. Key must be established, as an aural fact, by the exhibition and manipulation of its primary elements, and the centripetal force of the key center must be affirmed and exploited.

What follows is a possibility so vast that it has created the central technical preoccupation of Western music. The possibility of transposing materials from one pitch level to another is applied in practice to the transposition of harmonic elements from one key to another in the course of a single musical composition, or development of a musical idea. This process, of moving from one key center to another, is known as modulation. If key itself is the central principle of unity in traditional music, modulation may be said to introduce the principle of variety or contrast.

Further, modulation, through its extended application, is actually the basis for the elaboration in time (length) of Western composition, since it requires an extent of time in which to be established and perceived. It thus constitutes one of the bases on which an art of large dimensions could be developed.

Some of the technical and esthetic problems of key (tonality) and of modulation will be discussed in Part II. For the moment it is enough to point out that the traditional practice of key change or contrast, involving modulation from one key to another, assumes that the hearer is able to distinguish one pitch level from another. For it must be remembered that the internal pitch relations (including harmonic relations) of one key are exactly the same as those of any other. We may, in fact, take any composition (the Bach Prelude, for example, that will be mentioned below) and move the entire work up or down in pitch without altering its design. (It is interesting to observe that few listeners will be aware that this has been done. Only those with absolute pitch—the ability to identify a note by its absolute physical sound, without relation to another note—can be entirely sure on this count.) The ability to distinguish one pitch level from another need not be conscious, and in fact it seldom is except among trained musicians; but it is as important, as Tovey points out, as an appreciation of the conventions of perspective in the consideration of Renaissance painting. Tovey emphasizes "the enormous amount of collateral evidence that composers with a fine sense of tonality bring to bear upon the listener before they expect him to recognize that a piece of music has returned to its home tonic from a distance." (*The Mainstream of Music*, p. 167.)

By following up the central idea of the establishment of a pitch level or center—defined as a key—and the corollary idea of the possibility of changing from one key to another, we glimpse the basic mechanism of design in traditional music. If within a single scale or key the relation of the fifth (dominant) to the fundamental (tonic) is conceived as primary, we can easily extend the scope of this relation to embrace *sections* of a musical composition in the *keys* of the tonic and the dominant. It is obvious at once that an extension of time must be involved in order to establish the sense of each key, and to establish the relationship of one to the other. It is obvious also that this type of design, involving establishment, change, and return, is the genesis of a *form*. It is, as in Aristotle's definitions of Tragedy, the simple idea of Beginning, Middle, and End, the *locus classicus* of esthetics for all arts involving time.

We may now digress for a moment to consider a familiar piece of music (the first Prelude of Bach's *Well-Tempered Clavier*, Appendix, No. 1) that constitutes a simple, but almost complete, illustration of the basic principles of syntax and design in the harmonic tradition. This short piece demonstrates (among other things) the essence of the harmonic relationships that constitute our concept of tonality. A thorough analysis of the piece must, of course, be postponed until a useful vocabulary has been established; but, assuming that the reader has heard (or can play) this work, certain generalizations can be made even at this stage.

First, we understand this piece as a well-ordered succession of harmonies. We note, moreover, that these harmonies are deployed in a repetitive pattern; no chord or harmony is struck as a simultaneously sounding group. The notes of the harmony follow one another; they are set in motion in time, but they are still understood by the ear as forming themselves into units. The regularity of division and measurement further assures us of this.

Second, we feel the unity of the piece in a harmonic sense. It begins with a triad on C, and it ends with a triad on C. We feel that the harmonies in between relate to C, even though we cannot at this stage make an analysis of them. But we must sense, even at this stage, that the tonality of the work, even its form and structure, depend on the orderly relationship among chordal sounds moving to and from a center or fixed point.

Third, we are aware that this is almost completely a harmonic piece, and consciously so. There is no melody, at least in the sense of there being a sustained single voice that is predominant. (One remembers Gounod's famous addition to this Prelude, which is, for better or worse, a "melody." Writing a "melody" to the "accompaniment" of this Prelude was for many years a standard assignment at the Paris Conservatory; Gounod's is simply the most famous. Whether or not one deplores Gounod's *Ave Maria*—as is customary today—the exercise itself is not entirely without point, and does not deserve the sneers it usually attracts.)

As a harmonic piece, the Prelude seems planned to undertake the demonstration of the essential relationships that constitute our conception of tonality. It contains triads formed on five of the seven degrees of the diatonic C-major scale, as well as a variety of the most common seventh chords. It demonstrates with considerable clarity that the key of C major does in fact include all twelve tones of the chromatic scale (they are all present in this brief piece). The Prelude also poses the problem of modulation, as a basis for further consideration. (It is said by some that it modulates to G at measure 6, and back to C at measure 12; others state that it remains in C throughout.) If one can see the problem on this scale, one can by extension learn to consider modulation in its larger aspects.

Fourth, the Prelude calls our attention to several considerations having to do with speed, both absolute and relative, and with duration or length. The absolute speed at which this Prelude must be performed was not specified by Bach, but to any sensitive ear it must remain within certain limits entirely on the internal evidence of its harmonic design and flow. One should consider why Bach repeats each chord; why the duration as well as the relative length of each sound is important. It is necessary that the ear should set and adjust comfortably. In a sense, the first sound of the chord (first half of each measure) is arrival; the repetition (second half of each measure) is point of departure. Seldom in music do we find an example of such perfect clarity; but that clarity, it must be remembered, is exactly what Bach had in mind.

The beauty of this small piece is most manifest in its almost mathematical demonstration of the workings of a logical system. (In this connection, the advanced student may compare similar attempts by some of Bach's predecessors and contemporaries, as well as Bach's own earlier versions of the same piece, notably in the *Notebook for Wilhelm Friedemann Bach.*) Such a work as this Prelude is obviously not an "inspiration"; it is the result of thought and perfected art applied to a tradition. It is the idealization of the harmonic *schema;* and it is not coincidence or accident that it stands at the very opening of the *Well-Tempered Clavier.* It is the explanation, or the *argumentum,* of the entire work. The C-major Prelude is, in fact, a basic text for the study of traditional Western harmony; one might almost say that little else in the way of text ought to be required. It illustrates, in sum, that harmony is the governing principle of traditional organization in music, and that it is the combination of the several aspects of harmony that gives the music of the 18th and 19th centuries its unique quality, and its place among the highest achievements of human imagination.

The generalizations above, derived from the C-major Prelude, are important ones, to be considered carefully before undertaking a study of the working techniques involved. And it is to be stressed again that the idea of harmony, far from being a matter of connecting one triad to another in a schematic fashion, must include the ideas, as the Prelude clearly shows, of harmony as *sound* (its actual pitch, quality, mass, and intensity), of harmony as *motion* (duration, speed, deployment), and of harmony as *function* (the logical relation of part to part, and of parts to the whole).

There is perhaps but one further point of importance to be made by way of introduction, or as preparation for the study of the detailed technical aspects of harmony. That point necessitates a return to the consideration of time itself, which is the element in which harmony evolves and music exists. The operation of traditional harmony as an effective language of intelligible structure depends on a highly developed synthetic ability on the part not only of those who speak the language, but also of those who can claim to understand it.

Harmony as sound requires a simple degree of perception; it remains in the realm of sensation. Harmony as motion demands the further perceptive ability, and the beginnings of a synthetic power, to gather and assort elements into groups (the arpeggio into the chord; the broken figure into its structural unity). Harmony as function demands still more: it requires the synthetic ability to recollect and to anticipate in terms of an established and understood norm. This is already an extremely sophisticated acquisition of the intellect and the sensibilities, and it is, of course, impossible without the background of a long and highly developed tradition. The understanding of music, in this sense, is learned, like language, in childhood, through hearing, or perhaps, like a second language, later in life by those sufficiently interested and capable. But it is learned, and developed, as is the use of language, from rudimentary speech to the highest flights of rhetorical imagination, in which the demands on attention and comprehension are also essentially synthetic, and in which an effort of the mind is required to make a whole of successive related parts.

In the progress of a harmonic succession, the ear retains and anticipates. It moves, without conscious effort, freely in time, forward to what it expects, and backwards to what it remembers, only thus giving to the actually present sound its beauty and its meaning. Otherwise music becomes, as Santayana suggested, nothing more than a collection of unconnected sensations or "a drowsy reverie interrupted by nervous thrills."

Santayana points out (*Reason in Art*, Chapter 4) that "The process we undergo in mathematical or dialectical thinking is called understanding, because natural sequence is there adequately translated into ideal terms." Sound, he continues, "approaches this kind of ideality," for in music too "logical connections seem to be internally justified." Music "deploys a sensuous harmony by a sort of dialectic, suspending and resolving it, so that the parts become distinct and their relation vital." Santayana pursues the idea of the elaboration of abstract relations in time, and concludes that there is a limit to the extent to which elaboration may be carried. It "often exceeds the synthetic power of all but the best trained minds." "Both in scope and in articulation," he concludes, "musical faculty varies prodigiously."

Training in music, and specifically in the disciplines of traditional harmony, must be directed towards the development of ear and mind so that harmonic logic becomes apparent and so that form becomes whole. The study of harmony should develop the understanding so that relatively complex types of elaboration become intelligible, and so that the apprehension of syntax may become the basis of awareness of style or idiosyncrasy. The advantage of the trained ear and mind is the extension of their field of operation in time, and their increased power of synthesis.

It is towards the goal of such cultivation that the following chapters are directed.

Part One

Chapter One

Scales and Triads

Extension in Time of a Triad

Non-harmonic Tones

A Note on Figured Bass

SCALES AND TRIADS

Traditional theory has made Western music dependent on a concept of scales, major and minor, and on a pattern of triads built on the steps of these scales. But it soon becomes obvious that these abstractions or concepts are only relatively valid, and that musical practice is bound to them very loosely.

The minor scale or mode has always been an embarrassment to theorists. Tovey puts the matter simply when he says that "the minor scale is so unstable that the evidence of its common chords is conflicting and misleading." We shall have to return to this problem below. Meanwhile it should be observed that the common chords of the major scale are not as schematically simple as traditional theory would have them, nor is the major scale itself. Music itself seems to demonstrate the hypothesis that major and minor are, in fact, not completely separate and distinct in practice.*

---

* Busoni, in *Sketch of a New Esthetic of Music,* observes that "when we recognize that major and minor form one Whole . . . we arrive unconstrainedly at a perception of the Unity of our system of keys. . . . *We possess one single key.*"

15

Traditionally, the major scale is set forth as follows:

Ex. 1

The student is shown that on each of these notes of the scale it is possible to build a triad. Thus:

Ex. 2

These triads are identified, usually by Roman numerals, as I, II, III, and so on, and are described as being major or minor. In addition to the numeral designation, it has been usual to identify these seven scale steps and their triads as follows:

        I   —   Tonic (major)
       II   —   Supertonic (minor)
      III   —   Mediant (minor)
       IV   —   Subdominant (major)
        V   —   Dominant (major)
       VI   —   Submediant (minor)
      VII   —   Leading-tone (diminished)

As a starting point in elementary theory, it is usually stated that these triads, centering on the tonic, define a *key* or tonality. Thus, the triads above (Ex. 2) would be those occurring in the key of C major. It is true that a simple piece in C major will normally begin and end with the major triad on C, which is defined or established as the *tonic*, will make frequent use of the dominant, and will employ triads on the other steps of the scale as set out above. But musical practice must convince us at once that this schema is an over-simplification, and that it should be more practical for the student to begin immediately on a broader basis. Examination of a few simple pieces from the Classical or Romantic periods will demonstrate, for example, that:

a)   the supertonic, or II chord, is often major (that is, with raised third)
b)   the subdominant, or IV chord, is often minor (that is, with lowered third)
c)   tonic, mediant, and submediant are variable in mode (major or minor)

Skipping ahead momentarily, the student may observe that even in simple and short pieces chords will occur—*without weakening the sense of key*—that are not based on the seven steps of the scale. Thus, in C major, we may find triads (major or minor) on Db, Bb, Ab, etc. This phenomenon will be explored more fully in a later chapter. For the moment, the student will note the following schema, and apply it to major scales beginning on D, E, F, etc.

Ex. 3

I   II   III   IV   V   VI   VII

*less common

Thus we assume at the beginning the variability of mode in each common triad built on the steps of the major scale. It will be noted that the VII chord does not commonly occur in its simple or root position. Piston's definition of the VII chord as a dominant seventh chord (see below, Chapter II, page 40) lacking its root may be accepted provisionally. The VII chord (or V^0_7, in Piston's terminology) usually occurs in its *first inversion*, that is, with its third as lowest note.

All of the triads, major or minor, are used, in musical works, both in root position and in first inversion. In many traditional harmony books, it is stated that these triads also may occur in *second inversion*, that is, with the fifth as the lowest note. The second inversion is, however, usually a function of movement, and cannot be considered a static chord position. For the present, the student will disregard it entirely.

Ex. 4

root position   1st inversion   2nd inversion   1st inversion
                                                                 (open position)

From the schema above (Ex. 3), we may infer one fact of paramount importance: that is, in the key of C major, illustrated, the notes Eb, F♯, G♯, Ab, Bb, and C♯ may commonly occur. Both harmonically and melodically, a key based on any given note includes and employs notes not in the simple diatonic scale.

The minor scale is, as has been noted, unstable in its formation. Conventionally, it is given in several forms: harmonic, ascending melodic, and descending melodic.

Ex. 5

"harmonic" minor   Ascending "melodic" minor   Descending "melodic" minor

In practice, these forms are neither distinct nor real. The sound that distinguishes minor mode in the 18th and 19th centuries is basically that of the minor triad on the tonic and on the subdominant. As with the major, the dominant in minor is almost invariably a major triad. All other triads are variable, as they are in major, and again it must be pointed out that these variations not only lend scope to the imaginations of composers, but tend to eliminate sharp conventional distinctions of major and minor.

Traditionally, the triads of the harmonic minor are set forth in the same manner that has been used for the major. Thus:

I   —   Tonic (minor)
II   —   Supertonic (diminished)
III   —   Mediant (major) (augmented)
IV   —   Subdominant (minor)
V   —   Dominant (major)
VI   —   Submediant (major)
VII   —   Leading-tone (diminished)

Ex. 6

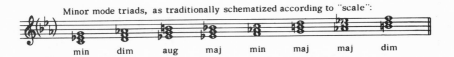

Minor mode triads, as traditionally schematized according to "scale":

min   dim   aug   maj   min   maj   maj   dim

The peculiarities of this conventionalizing are almost too many, and too unreal, to detail. In most systems, the triad on III is given as an augmented triad (in C minor, E♭—G—B♮). In practice this triad does not often occur. The triads formed on II, III, VI, and VII are so variable as to make hardly worth while an attempt at schematizing any basic form.

For the moment, the student will be well advised to observe in the music of Haydn, Mozart, Bach, and Beethoven the sound and construction of minor chordal progressions. For his own exercises at this time, he will be confined to tonic triad (minor) and dominant (major), which at least avoid confusion. The student will also note, however, that when diminished triads *do* occur, on a II root (and they do), they are used almost always (like the VII in major) in first inversion. Reasons for this will become apparent at a later stage.

EXTENSION IN TIME OF A TRIAD

The triad assumes a variety of forms in music. It is perhaps least often found as a vertical combination of three notes, as it exists in the schemas given above. Doublings in various octaves of the three notes of the triad, varieties of spacing, differences of register or texture all occur. These do not affect the harmonic character of the triad as regards its function, although they certainly affect the sound. For example, taking the triad C–E–G as the tonic of C major, we may find the following, among a multiplicity of other possibilities:

Ex. 7

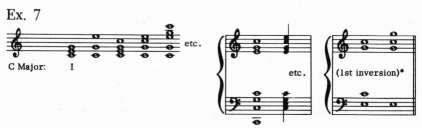

*When 3rd is in bass (1st inversion) it is common practice <u>not</u> to use the third again in upper voices. There are, however, innumerable exceptions.

The triad may also occur as a non-simultaneous sounding of three notes. Common examples are the arpeggio and the Alberti bass pattern:

Ex. 8 a. Clementi: Sonatina, Op. 36, No. 1

b. Mozart: Piano Sonata, K. 545

c. Schubert: Impromptu, Op. 142, No. 2

d. Mozart: London Notebook, K. 15d

Examples of the Alberti bass and of arpeggiated simple triads will be found in the Clementi Sonatina (Appendix, No. 3) and in the well-known C-major Sonata of Mozart (K. 545).

It is important that the student begin to recognize and handle triads in this way at the very beginning. The four-part style (based on the chorales of Bach) is only one way of approaching harmonic sound and connection, and although it has been used pedagogically for centuries, it remains a limited, and in some respects inhibiting, approach to harmony.

For harmony is not only identification and connection of chords; it is a matter of deploying sounds in a time continuum, of giving motion to chordal sounds, of manipulating the notes of the triad horizontally (or melodically) as well as vertically.

Thus, the student should begin at once making simple experiments with one triad, along the lines indicated.

The student should avoid placing the fifth in the bass; otherwise he is free to exercise his imagination. The student will also seek additional relevant examples of extending the sound of a single triad in the music of Mozart, Bach, Beethoven, and other composers. (See, for example, the Schubert *Moment musical*, Appendix, No. 7.)

It will become apparent that the prolongation of the sound of a triad in this way will soon create a feeling of stability as regards harmonic sound. In other words, although the simple triad C–E–G sounded once or twice as a simultaneous chord gives no clue as to its function or identification, the prolonged sounding of the triad will create the impression of C as a tonal center, for the ear tends to interpret a repeated triad as either a tonic or a dominant sound. This is a fact of cardinal importance. We may re-state it in the following terms: tonality (or rather, the establishment of the sense of tonality) depends on a time factor as well as on the factor of harmonic or triadic relationship.

Exercise:
The student will attempt to "compose" a piece, 8 measures in length (or longer if possible), using only a single triad.

The student will find this exercise difficult because of the very limited possibilities open to him. But by imagination in creating a figural pattern, in using the resources of the piano or other instruments, by indicating tempo, dynamics, and all expressive nuances, it will be found possible to write a short musical "composition" not entirely devoid of sense or interest.

NON-HARMONIC TONES

A musical passage (or exercise) based on a single triad may become more interesting through the use of *non-harmonic tones*, which may be defined simply as notes not found in the triad forming the harmonic foundation of the passage. Thus, if the C-major triad (C–E–G) is the fundamental harmonic unit heard, the notes, D, F, A, and B may occur melodically as "non-harmonic" tones in relation to that triad.

The simplest form of non-harmonic tone is known as the passing tone, which is usually found as a connecting tone between two notes that form part of the triad. Thus the note D may be heard as a passing tone between C and E, or the note F between E and G. Passing tones are described as accented or unaccented as they occur on strong or weak beats of the measure, or as they are relatively stronger or weaker rhythmically than the chord tones they connect. Thus:

Ex. 9a.

b. Mozart: Piano Sonata in C, K. 309

c. Mozart: Piano Sonata in C, K. 309

Two passing tones may also occur simultaneously in different voices, as in the following:

Ex. 10   L. Mozart: Menuet from Notebook for W. A. Mozart

In conventionalized patterns of the traditional period, such as scale passages, the variable placing of accented and unaccented passing tones makes for rhythmic flexibility and variety:

Ex. 11

Another simple form of non-harmonic tone is the neighboring tone, also called embellishment or auxiliary tone. The neighboring tone is a note that embellishes a chord tone by stepwise departure (whole or half step) and immediate return. Neighboring tones also may be accented or unaccented:

Ex. 12

Schubert: *Wiener Damenländler*, Op. 67

Mozart: Allegro, K. 9a

C: I

The accented passing tone is sometimes described as an appoggiatura,* on the grounds that all passing tones by definition must be rhythmically weak. The same nomenclature would presumably have to be applied to the accented neighboring tone. The appoggiatura, however, is more commonly defined as a non-harmonic tone occurring on a strong beat, but approached by a melodic skip:

Ex. 13

The appoggiatura note may be of relatively long or short duration, but it is always strongly accented, and in the traditional practice most often resolves by step to a chord tone. A repeated note may, in context, become an appoggiatura:

Ex. 14

---

* See, for example, Piston, *Harmony* (1st ed., 1941), p. 103ff.

† The simple appoggiatura (or accented passing tone) was generally written thus in the 18th century, among other reasons so that chord-tone and non-harmonic tone were clearly distinguished.

It is to be emphasized that the terminology is less important than the understanding of the function of the non-harmonic tone in question in any given instance. Passing and neighboring tones, accented or unaccented, as well as appoggiaturas, require little further explanation. In general, non-harmonic tones may be merely connective, even decorative, exerting little or no pull away from the harmonies they embellish (as in obviously unaccented passing or neighboring tones), or they may, by position, duration, or accent, call attention to themselves and create a tension with relation to the underlying harmony. The manipulation of these tones therefore requires a sense of harmonic firmness and balance; the non-harmonic tone must clearly appear to be what it is, and must not by either its emphasis or its duration seem to demand a change of harmony. Thus, for example, the following, if played very slowly, might well appear to imply a change of chord (to the dominant) under the D:

Ex. 15

The same notes at a quick tempo do not create the same impression.

We thus are able to infer a second fact of importance: the sense of harmonic relation, change, or effect depends on *speed* (or tempo) as well as on the relative duration of single notes or triadic units. Both absolute time (measurable length and speed) and relative time (proportion and division) must at all times be taken into account in harmonic thinking or analysis.

Before proceeding to the following exercise, the student should examine pieces given in the Appendix to this volume, identifying non-harmonic tones of various types, and should do the same with simple pieces of his own random choosing.

Exercise:

The student will proceed to "compose" a phrase, or perhaps even a very short complete piece, again using only a single triad as harmonic material, but freely using non-harmonic tones of the types described above.

In making these attempts, the student should experiment with differing textures and chord figurations.

The following examples of using a single triad in an extended way may be of some value as suggestions for the above exercise:

Ex. 16   Mozart: Theme and Variations, K. 500

A. Scarlatti: Toccata V

It is also suggested that the student examine a piano reduction of the first pages of the Prelude to *Das Rheingold* of Wagner, and listen to the orchestral version in any good recording. This is perhaps the most notable example in music of a lengthy passage in which a single harmony (an Eb-major triad) is used.

A NOTE ON FIGURED BASS

The student will encounter what is known as figured bass, both functionally in Baroque music, and pedagogically as a means of identifying inversions of chords.

The principle involved is simple: the figure (or figures) placed under or over the bass note give the important interval *from the bass note* that must appear in the chord.

Thus, a chord in first inversion is identified by a 6, indicating that one of the notes of the triad must be a sixth higher than the bass note. If, as in this instance, which is among the most common of figurations, only one number is given, it is understood that the remaining note will be a third higher than the bass note. Actually, the figure 6 is an abbreviation for the figures $\frac{6}{3}$, the 3 being understood.

By the same procedure, the second inversion of the triad is identified by the figures $\frac{6}{4}$.

Sharp, flat, or natural signs may be used with the numerals, indicating that they are raised or lowered with reference to the simple scale tones otherwise required. A sharp, flat, or natural appearing without a numeral will always refer to the third from the bass note.

When no numeral is given, a root position is understood, that is, the intervals $\frac{5}{3}$ (a fifth and a third) from the bass note.

Chapter Two

Tonic and Dominant

The Dominant Seventh Chord

Harmony in Two, Three, Four, or More Parts

TONIC AND DOMINANT

The first *triadic* relation of importance—and, in fact, the fundamental triadic relationship of all—is that of dominant and tonic. It would not be an exaggeration to state that all traditional Western music is built on extensions of this relationship.

The student will have heard the formula dominant-tonic (or V–I) thousands of times in musical works. Just as compositions normally close on a tonic (or I) triad, so this triad is normally preceded by a dominant (or V) chord. The feeling of closing, or cadence, that this succession gives us is a basic element in the design of Western music.

At this point, it should be emphasized that the force of the dominant, that is, our sense that it requires resolution, or movement towards a tonic, is arbitrary. It rests on no law of acoustics, but is an acquired meaning. It is the single most important fact in what we shall call the *syntax* of music. Our ears have accepted this meaning and this necessity for some hundreds of years. But other periods, and other cultures, have used other formulas. A cadence of the 14th century, for example (and we must assume that for

30

14th-century ears it had the same meaning of finality as V–I does for us), was this:

Ex. 17   Landini

Much modern music also relies on other conventions of force, direction, connection, and finality.

The root positions of dominant and tonic triads may be found in the schemas of the preceding chapter. Any triad (major or minor) may be chosen as a tonic; the dominant triad (almost invariably major) will be the triad whose root is a fifth above or a fourth below the root of the first triad. Thus:

Ex. 18

The relationship of these triads may be ambiguous, especially in a schematic formulation. Thus, particularly in the following position, with the fifth of the presumed tonic in the top voice, either triad may be heard as the tonic:

Ex. 19

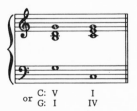

It becomes apparent immediately that the definition of function depends on the musical context: to be exact, on the ear's assurance of the static or final quality of the I chord functioning as tonic or point of rest. Normally, this assurance depends on the I chord or tonic being established as a point of departure as well as a point of arrival or finality.

Our musical formula can therefore not be simply V to I, but must be extended, as the very beginning of meaningful relationship, to I–V–I. The idea of key or tonality presupposes both a point of departure and an identical point of arrival.

The first musical problems in the manipulation of even this simple formula involve considerations beyond their note-to-note connection: *time* (extension, duration, speed) and *rhythm* (placement, pulse, meter, accent).

While all of the complexities of temporal and rhythmic relationships cannot be explored at this early stage, the function of the barline must be considered here. The first beat (or downbeat) of a measure is not only stress; it is also, generally, repose. When a feeling of finality is desired, the normal rhythmic relationship of dominant to tonic is therefore usually that of *resolution* on the downbeat or, grammatically, of dominant to tonic across the barline.

Ex. 20

The V chord, or dominant, will often occur, as will all other triads, in its first inversion:

Ex. 21   Clementi: Sonatina, Op. 36, No. 3

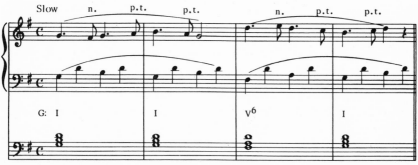

(harmonic basis)

Through study of musical examples, the student will note the usual procedures of connection or voice-movement involved in moving from a I chord to a V, or a V to a I. Completely parallel movement (that is, all notes of a chord moving in the same direction to the next chord) is generally avoided. Minimum movement is, in the simplest styles, often employed: that is, movement of a note of one chord to the *nearest* note of the following. When one tone is common to both chords, it is the usual practice, and the simplest, to retain it. In moving from V to I, the dynamic qualities of the notes of the V chord are taken into account: the third of the V chord (being the leading-tone) usually (but not invariably) moves to the tonic; the fifth of the V chord (being the supertonic) usually, but again not invariably, also moves to the tonic. At a final V–I cadence, the root of the V chord moves to the root of the I.

The common practices of voice-leading should be apparent to any student with a musical ear, and should be mastered by all students without difficulty. When exceptions are found (as they are in all composers) the student should try to discern the musical reasons for each.

In examining simple pieces of the Classical period, the student will have noted occasional occurrences of the I chord in its second inversion, usually preceding the V chord, and especially at the close of a phrase or section. We can now suggest that this chord, rather than being a tonic or I chord, with the fifth in the bass, is in effect a V or dominant chord, with two accented upper neighbor or passing tones, and that the fifth of the scale in the bass is the true root. The sound of the I_4^6 is always unstable in this context, and the chord clearly seems to function as an aspect of the dominant rather than of the tonic. It is suggested that the student so consider it when it is found in this form in cadences.

THE DOMINANT SEVENTH CHORD

The student who has looked at much music, or listened with attention, will have discovered that in music of the Classical and Romantic periods the V chord will often appear as a *seventh chord*: that is, a chord with an additional third added to the basic triad, making the total spread of the chord from root to upper note the interval of a seventh:

Ex. 22

Dominant 7th

This chord occurring on V is the *dominant seventh chord*. The addition of the fourth note (which is also the fourth degree of the scale) gives added force to the characteristic sound of the dominant, and, because the fourth degree has a strong tendency to move to the third, strengthens its drive towards resolution in the tonic. The implications of this drive are among the basic structural forces in our music. Simple experiment, at the keyboard or with other instruments, or simple listening to V^7–I constructions, will persuade the student that the demand of the V^7 for resolution is, *to our ears*, almost inescapably compelling. The dominant seventh is, in fact, the central propulsive force in our music; it is unambiguous and unequivocal.

The progression I–V–I (or I–V^7–I) is, as has been stated at the opening of this chapter, the fundamental harmonic relationship in our traditional music. Further than that, it may be said to be the genesis of all *form* in our music. The student will find many pieces in the Classical period in which the formula I–V–I forms the entire harmonic basis of a phrase or even of a short piece. The simplest two-part form often consists of a movement, protracted over four or eight measures, from I to V, followed by a matching movement of return from V to I. Thus:

> I: V
>
>   (X number of measures, often eight)
>
> V: I

Simple three-part forms are often extensions of the formula I–V–I prolonged over eight-measure phrases. Thus:

> I: .... (I)
>
> V: .... (V)
>
> I: I

The following three examples may be studied carefully. The student should, on his own initiative, find other examples of a similar type.

Ex. 23a.   L. Mozart: Polonaise, Notebook for W. A. Mozart

b.   Mozart: German Dances, K. 590, No. 6

*See Chapter III

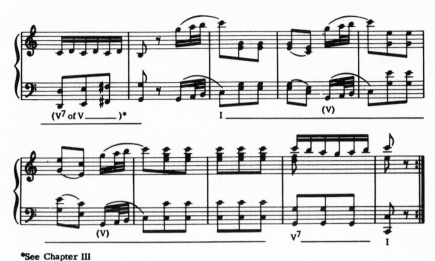

*See Chapter III

c. Schubert: Waltz, Op. 9b

The differences in deployment of V and I harmonies in the above examples should be carefully noted. In the Leopold Mozart (Ex. 23a), the fundamental design is:

$$\tfrac{3}{4}: \quad I - - \mid I - - \mid I - - \mid V - - \mid I$$

In the first two measures there is what amounts essentially, in terms of over-all harmonic design, to a subdivision of I–V–I. This type of design should be studied with attention. It is capable of great extension and development, as will clearly be seen in pieces of more complex type. But the principle here exposed is a fundamental one of musical form and design.

The German Dance of W. A. Mozart (Ex. 23b) shows a longer extension of the I triad through the first eight measures, as this is balanced by a second eight-measure phrase employing an equal extension of V. Thus:

$$\tfrac{3}{8} \quad \text{I} \; . \quad . \mid . \quad . \mid . \quad . \mid . \quad . \mid . \quad . \mid . \quad . \text{V} \; . \quad . \mid \text{I}$$

Subdivisions in which V is heard or suggested occur in unaccented upbeats or anacruses (at the opening and in full measures 2 and 4), and in the next-to-last measure, which is also an anacrusis, but on a more extended scale. But the first eight measures in their entirety are heard essentially as a prolonged I, just as the second phrase of eight measures—with similar subdivisions—is heard as a prolonged V. The final phrase of course repeats the first one, creating a balanced and symmetrical simple form.

The Schubert (Ex. 23c) shows another type of I–V–I design. There are no harmonic subdivisions within the measure. What is to be noted here is the symmetrical balance of two four-measure phrases within an eight-measure unit:

$$\tfrac{3}{4} : \quad \text{I} \; . \; . \mid \text{V} \; . \; . \mid \text{V} \; . \; . \mid \text{I} \; . \; . \mid \text{I} \; . \; . \mid \text{V} \; . \; . \mid \text{V} \; . \; . \mid \text{I}$$

The student will also observe how the accompanying chords are disposed in the simplest and clearest manner possible with respect to voice-leading.

The history of the dominant seventh (and of all other seventh chords) in Western music is interesting and relevant at this point.

We now accept the sound of the dominant seventh as a matter of course, and although it is not a sound that implies rest, it does not seem to our ears to be harsh or particularly dissonant. Yet it was for centuries considered a dissonance, and its use was governed by carefully calculated procedures covering its introduction and resolution. Monteverdi is usually credited with being the first composer to use the dominant seventh without preparation or, in other words, to use it as an independent harmonic unit rather than as a resultant of linear motion among melodic voices. In any case, by the 18th century the independence of the dominant seventh may be said to have been established. This independence has important consequences. If the dominant seventh is taken as a real unit, rather than as a triad with an additional dissonant tone, then it acquires stability with relation to other notes functioning as non-harmonic tones, just as does a simple triad. With a four-note complex (G–B–D–F in the key of C) it is clear that there are only three notes of the diatonic scale remaining (C, E, A), which will be non-harmonic. These, however, are used in the same manner as they would be in relation to a triad.

Ex. 24   C. M. von Weber: *Sonett*, Op. 23, No. 4

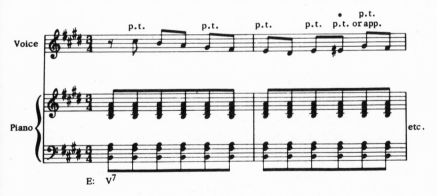

* Note that chromatically raised or lowered notes (not in the simple diatonic scale) may be freely used as passing or neighboring tones.

Certain ambiguities occur at once. As a dominant harmony is deployed in time, it may not be clear whether a simple dominant harmony or a dominant seventh harmony will be heard. In the Clementi (Ex. 21 above), to take an instance, the seventh does not occur until the end of the third measure, where it occurs, in fact, as what may be interpreted as a passing tone.

How we hear this will depend on tempo, accent, and context. It is not important that we classify the sound analytically; it is important only that our ears establish a relation, and that we understand that this is a manipulation of a rather subtle kind. Once this is understood, on this rather simple plane, we have made a large step towards appreciating further subtleties of harmonic design as they are employed by skilled composers. The principle here is simply one of *delay*.

There is one other aspect of the dominant seventh chord that must be noted: it often occurs in incomplete form, with only three notes, either the third or the fifth being omitted:

Ex. 25

Where only the seventh itself occurs with the root, one normally understands a dominant seventh harmony. (See the Clementi Sonatina, Appendix, No. 3, measure 36).

The root itself is frequently omitted, leaving the diminished triad (B–D–F in C), almost always in its first inversion (D as lowest note). Although this may be described as a triad on the seventh degree of the scale, or VII chord, we can perhaps now see why it is possible and reasonable to consider it essentially as an incomplete V⁷. It is almost invariably dominant in function, although it does not often occur when a feeling of absolute close or finality is desired.

The dominant seventh (and other seventh chords) may also occur in various inversions, with the third, fifth, or seventh, rather than the root, in the bass. The dominant seventh of C (G–B–D–F) may thus be found in the following positions.

Ex. 26 *

1st   6   2nd   4   3rd   4   1st   2nd   3rd
       5   3   2

All of these inversions are freely used. The peculiarity of the third inversion (dearly beloved of Handel, and used with great effect in the entire Classical period) is that it almost invariably resolves to the first inversion of the tonic, the bass note (the fourth scale degree) moving almost irresistibly to the third scale degree:

Ex. 27

in C   in D   in B♭   etc.

One further phrase may now be cited, to be added to those given in Example 23, of the use of I–V–I, and in illustration of some of the further points noted above:

* The figures for these inversions, reading upward from the lowest note, as with the simple triad, to denote actual intervals, are:
first inversion—6–5–3 (often shortened to 6–5);
second inversion—6–4–3 (often shortened to 4–3);
third inversion—6–4–2 (almost always shortened to 4–2, or merely 2).

Ex. 28 Bach: Prelude in A♭ major, *Well-Tempered Clavier*, Book I

These few measures require the most careful study. Although harmonically they are no more complex than the phrases cited in Example 23, they exhibit a much greater sophistication and subtlety. It will be observed that in this phrase the structure is alternate: I–V–I–V–I. The V⁷ occurs in first inversion in the second measure, with the appearance of the actual seventh delayed until the second part of the measure. In the fourth measure (which is syntactically a simple V⁷ in root position) we are left in some doubt, since the root of the dominant is not actually heard until the third beat of the measure. But, since the lower voice in the second two measures repeats the upper voice of the first two, we have a notion of what to expect. Our ears await the E♭; our expectation has been aroused by the use of the repetitive pattern. We are thus able to anticipate, and to synthesize aurally.

HARMONY IN TWO, THREE, FOUR, OR MORE PARTS

Although a triad, by definition, consists of three notes, we have already seen that these notes may be doubled in various octaves, or deployed horizontally in a variety of figurations or textures. The effect of triadic harmony can be produced even when there are only two voices employed, or two notes sounding simultaneously, as in the little phrase of Clementi given as Example 18, or as in dozens of pieces by Bach, Handel, and innumerable other composers of the 18th and 19th centuries. (See also examples in Appendix.)

In two-part music for the piano, it should be borne in mind that the notes may be sustained through use of the pedal, and that in this way, through cumulative sounding, the full harmonies may be heard. But Bach, for example, did not have such a pedal on his keyboard instruments, nor is such a sustaining effect possible in two-part music for voices or diverse instruments; the effect of such carried-over tones, except as they are carried over in the listener's ear, should therefore be discounted. This exception, however, is a most important one. It is, in fact, one of the fundamental conditions of our understanding harmony. For harmony must be understood with the ear, rather than with the eye, and the ear is dependent on its recollection of previous sounds to make logical connection with present or anticipated ones. This point has been stressed in the Introduction, but it should be applied here with specific reference to the examples given in this chapter. These serve, it is hoped, to illustrate in a simple manner principles that are elaborately developed in larger works of music.

Conventional harmony pedagogy takes a four-voice texture (with all chords made immediately explicit) as its norm. The reasons given for this practice are not always entirely convincing. We have discussed (again in the Introduction) the fact that the four-part chorale style of Bach is a special style, not necessarily a norm. Aside from the questions of rhythm involved, examination of music of the traditional period will show us that—except for chorales, works for four-part chorus or for string quartet—writing in four parts is no more frequent than writing in two, three, or for that matter in five, six or eight parts.

The problems and practices of voice-leading are approximately the same with any number of voices. Voice-leading, in traditional practice, is simply the following in most cases of the natural tendencies of notes to move in a given direction (for example, leading-tone to tonic), and the construction of an interesting horizontal line in each voice of the harmony. But the definition of "interesting" is variable, and the exceptions to expected movement are innumerable. There is no judgment of quality possible except in terms of the ear itself, or in terms of what is appropriate in a given style.

Excessive parallelism in voice-leading is generally deplored. The ear at once persuades the student that parallel motion in most textures sounds weak. But, on the other hand, in some textures it may be deliberately employed.

Parallel fifths and octaves (that is, successive soundings of these intervals in the same two voices) are prohibited in most books that prescribe "rules." Such successions do weaken harmonic motion in many instances, and if used to excess tend to create the effect of one voice being eliminated, not only because of its lack of independence, but because the overtones tend to make the two separate sounds coalesce. The student therefore should use caution in such parallels, although he will find instances in Bach, Mozart, and Beethoven where they occur. He should not, however, interpret these instances as an absolute license for indiscretion.

In four-part harmony (whether chorale style or other) the persistent problem will often be: which note of the triad should be doubled? It is obvious that one of the three notes of the triad must be duplicated in order to maintain the fourth voice of the harmony. Here again, certain "rules" are often prescribed for the student. But the thoughtful study of a dozen pages of Bach or Mozart should enable the student to draw useful and musical conclusions for his own guidance, *insofar as the styles of these two composers are concerned.*

At some later point, the student should compare the usages of Bach with those of various 18th-, 19th-, and 20th-century composers. He will by then be able to conclude that "rules" concerning

doubling, spacing, voice-leading, and other matters, are not constant at all—that they are, in fact, *properties of style*, not of
grammar.

The student will, however, find certain practices commonly observed in the 18th and 19th centuries, and certain usages as normal
in Chopin (for example) as in Bach. One such practice concerns
the resolution of the dominant seventh chord. It is almost always
resolved normally—that is, to the tonic—with supertonic going to
tonic, fourth to third, and leading-tone to tonic. Of course there
are exceptions. Some of these, such as the resolution of the V^7 to
the VI, occur as normal procedures, and will be discussed in
Chapter VII. But the norms remain the same through most of
these two centuries, and even the departures from the norm depend on the acceptance of the norm for their *syntactical* meaning
and their *auditory* effect. Basically, what occurs in Chopin and
Wagner and later composers is a matter of *delay* in the resolution:
that is, a matter of deployment in time. (See Chapters VIII, IX,
and X.)

Exercise:

The student will "compose" several phrases, in varying
figurations, and one complete "piece" of eight measures,
using the formulas I–V–I and I–V^7–I. Non-harmonic tones
may be used freely.

Chapter Three

The Extension of the Dominant-Tonic Relationship

The II and II⁷ Chords

Contrapuntal Factors

THE EXTENSION OF THE
DOMINANT-TONIC RELATIONSHIP

At the beginning of Chapter II it was stated that the extension of the dominant-tonic relationship forms the basis of structure and meaning in all traditional music. It is now time to examine the first processes of this mechanism.

The principle is essentially simple. If the tonic triad represents the beginning and ending of a conventional musical structure, that is, its static or fixed points, the dominant may be said to represent a dynamic or moving force tending always towards the tonic. It may appear that this principle is capable of extension, and indeed musical practice proves that it is so. *Another triad may function in a dominant relation to the dominant itself.* This triad bears the same relationship to the dominant as the dominant bears to the tonic: it is the triad whose root is a fourth lower (or a fifth higher) than that of the dominant; in other words, the triad based on the supertonic, or the II chord, *major, minor, or diminished.*

We thus have a further syntactical structure, II–V–I, which serves as the conventional cadence of music in its traditional period.*

THE II AND II⁷ CHORDS

The II chord may be defined as a dominant once removed, in terms of its relationship to the tonic. This descriptive term may help clarify its function and explain some of its uses. But a further word of explanation is necessary. It was noted in Chapter II that the dominant itself (that is, the V or V⁷) is almost invariably major. Yet we see that the II chord, if based on the notes of the conventional major scale, will be a minor triad, and if based on the conventional minor scale will be a diminished triad. In the music of the masters from Bach through Brahms, however, harmonic practice is not as simple as that; harmonic thought is not based entirely on the "fixed" scales. Major, minor, and diminished triads all occur on the second degree of any scale, mode, or key, and they are used freely and interchangeably. It is therefore not necessary to call a major triad on II an "altered" chord, as has been the practice in much pedagogic terminology; such a triad is simply one of the possibilities regularly existing and employed.

The student or reader may hesitate to accept this view without supporting evidence. It is therefore of the utmost importance that at this point he study carefully, either alone or with the guidance of an instructor, a variety of classical compositions, with particular attention to the mode and use of the triad or seventh chord based on the supertonic. He will find that the II chord often occurs with

* The traditional cadence is often given as IV–V–I. This odd misconception has persisted. A discussion of the IV and its function will be found below (Chapter V), along with further observations about traditional cadence and style. The II chord is very frequently found in its first inversion, and is in fact usually so found in final cadences of the traditional period. The fact that the fourth degree of the scale (the third of the II chord) is the bass note in this case is probably the basis of the conventionalizing of the IV–V–I cadence definition. This is discussed more fully in Chapter V.

a major third, especially when leading to—or preceding—a half-close or phrase-ending on the dominant. But he will also find that it occurs in this form at many other points, including final cadences leading through V or V⁷ to the tonic.

The following four examples are taken from final cadences of four Bach chorales in *major* keys (published consecutively as Nos. 154, 155, 156, and 157, Breitkopf edition), and show four *different* (and common) forms of II–V–I:

Ex. 29

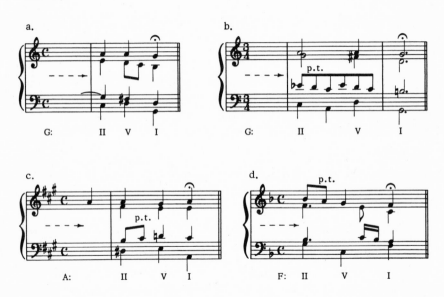

In (a) we have *minor* II in first inversion, with added seventh.

In (b) we have, in a major key, a *diminished* II in first inversion, with added seventh. (Conventional terminology often refers to this form as being "borrowed" from the minor. This is merely a way of trying to avoid the fact that major and minor are more mixed than is usually allowed.)

In (c) we have a *major* II in first inversion, with added
      seventh, leading to V⁷. (It will be noted that in (a)
      and (b), II leads to V with the seventh added to the
      V as a "passing tone.")
In (d) we have a *minor* II⁷ in root position.

The following may also be noted:

x=anticipating notes

Here we have a minor II, in first inversion, with added seventh,
followed by V without seventh.

From these examples, it is apparent that there exists a fascinating
variety of possibilities in the use of the progression II–V–I. It is
evident that when the II chord occurs in its major form it functions as a true dominant of V. It is for this reason that Piston
characterizes this form as the V of V (or dominant of the dominant), a characterization that is eminently just and obviously sensible. But the II chord in its minor form is also dominant in
function with relation to the V. More accurately, it may be said
to lead to I *through* V. Its force in this form is very strong, hence
the possibility of describing it as a dominant once removed. What
we have here is again a consideration of the utmost importance, for
the difference in action or function of the minor II (as opposed
to the major II) is one of *degree* or *force*. It is this principle that
must be grasped if the dynamic nature of traditional harmony is to
be understood.

We have seen, and our ears will have proved to us indisputably, that we can increase the force of the dominant's drive towards resolution in the tonic by making the simple V chord into a V^7 chord. We can see, equally, that the drive of the II chord towards the V chord has several degrees of force. The force is increased by making the triad major. It is still further increased by adding the seventh to the major II chord, thus making it a true dominant seventh (V^7) of the dominant. An intermediate stage of force is represented by making the minor or diminished II a II^7 chord. This is, in fact, the commonest form of the II–(V)–I motion.

Examples of all forms of II–V–I cadences are extremely easy to find in the music of the 18th and 19th centuries. The student should note and collect such examples, and should study them carefully from the standpoints of motion, force, and timing, and especially from the standpoint of style. The following are typical simple examples:

Ex. 30 a. Clementi: Sonatina, Op. 36, No. 3

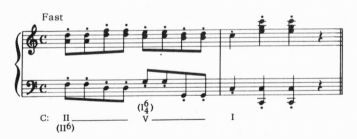

b. Mozart: Piano Concerto in G, K. 453

c. Haydn: Sonata, B & H 48

G: II⁶   I⁶₄   V⁷   I

d. Haydn: Sonata, B & H 41

Bb: I   II⁶   V⁷   I

e.   Handel   f.   Handel

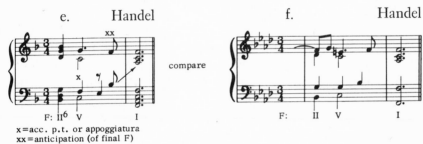

compare

F: II⁶ V   I   F: II   V   I

x = acc. p.t. or appoggiatura
xx = anticipation (of final F)

In (a) and (c) above, it will be noted that the I^6_4, discussed in Chapter II, occurs between II and V. This usage is very common. The dominant sound and function of the I^6_4 in this context is quite clear.

The student should at this point practice improvising at the keyboard, or writing out, passages in all keys based on the following schemes (all should be done in major and minor, and with varying kinds of II chords):

1) I–II⁶–V⁷–I
2) I–II⁶₅–V⁷–I
3) I–II⁶₅–I⁶₄–V (V⁷) –I
4) I–V–I–II⁶₅–I⁶₄–V (V⁷) –I

The fourth of these schemas may be described as a simple sta-
bilizing formula for tonality. Nothing more is needed to establish
the sense of key with complete firmness. It will be evident as a
corollary that it must be possible to construct complete pieces
using nothing further than this in the way of harmonic vocabulary.
The Leopold Mozart Polonaise is such a piece (see Appendix, No.
2), and a great quantity of others may be found very easily. From
the standpoint of "practical" harmony or keyboard improvisation,
the student will find indeed that almost any folk-style tune or
simple diatonic melody can be adequately "harmonized" using
nothing more than I, II, and V.

CONTRAPUNTAL FACTORS

The concept of force in the analysis and application of dominant
drives towards resolution may be difficult for the student to grasp
at this point. It is essential therefore that he begin to read carefully
(or analyze) a number of apparently simple traditional pieces, and
to listen carefully for the use and control of these forces in such
works. For the use and control of dominant propulsion are crucial
points in harmonic technique, and hence of traditional structure
and meaning in music.

The use of a major II instead of a minor II brings increased force
through the creation of a new leading-tone: the raised fourth
degree of the scale (in C major, F♯) which will very strongly demand (in our ears, that is) to proceed upward to the fifth or dominant. It is the creation of these new leading-tones that is the prime
operative factor in further extensions of this principle.

The leading-tone, the fourth degree, and the supertonic all have,
to our ears, strong tendencies to move in a given direction, particularly when they occur in a dominant seventh chord, explicit or
implied. In any case, they move in time, as melodic progressions,
and form continuities within any given texture. These tendencies
of notes produce *motion*, and motion in time is not only melody

and harmony, but counterpoint as well. It is, in fact, music itself.

The related movement of two or more voices is the simplest definition of counterpoint, which implies simultaneous opposition and unity of these voices. This movement is inseparable from any use or consideration of harmony, which also depends on motion, relation, and contrast.

Dominant harmony, as we have seen, usually resolves in the simplest and most direct manner to a tonic (whether this be V to I or II to V). The dominant seventh chord itself exercises a stronger aural force than most simple triads, and sets up, in our ears, an expectation of movement and resolution. The composer can manipulate this expectation; in fact, this is one of the elementary subtleties of musical composition or organization. He can delay the resolution, resolve it to a VI chord (see Chapter VII), or find other means of maintaining the interest and curiosity of the listener. But he will, almost invariably, eventually reach the tonic resolution that the listener awaits.

Other triads do not possess this type of drive towards an expected resolution, or possess it in lesser degree. From the static tonic triad, for example, one can proceed to almost any other harmony. This will be demonstrated in the following chapters. But here again, the movements of the component notes of the triad are *linear*; that is, they move in time and produce melodic motion. In short, the notes that form harmonies also move in a more or less contrapuntal fashion.

The linear movement of harmony is most clearly seen in a melody, especially when it occurs as the top voice or line of any musical unit. Melody in this sense may be said to be actually nothing more than a linear extension, elaboration, or variation of a harmonic movement. The argument as to whether melody comes first and (again, to our ears) implies harmony, or whether melody is a horizontal deployment of harmony, is centuries old. It has no answer, nor is it worth seeking one. Harmony and melody interact, and in traditional Western music are inseparable. Certainly, in many instances, one feels that melody follows a harmonic pattern. This is clear if one refers, for example, to the phrase of the Schubert Waltz cited in Chapter II (Ex. 23c), or to motifs such as the following:

Ex. 31 a.   Bach: Two-Part Invention, G major

b.   Haydn: Sonata, B & H 49

c.   Beethoven: Piano Sonata, Op. 2, No. 1

d. Rossini: "Cara immagine," from *The Barber of Seville*

In any case, linear movement occurs in all other voices of any harmonic sequence, whatever its texture. Or, conversely, one might say that harmonic change and movement occur through the progression of two or more melodic (or horizontal) lines. Harmony, as has been suggested above, may be defined by the action or interaction of only two voices. Such a texture, in fact, is at the root of harmonic development, for it establishes the polarity of top and bottom voices in musical movement.

Exercise:
    The student will compose two or three complete pieces (in different keys and in different figurations) using various forms of I–II–V–I. The pieces should consist of two balanced eight-measure phrases. The Leopold Mozart piece may be used as a model.

Supplementary Work:
    The student should examine other music in the Appendix, and seek out further examples in Beethoven, Schubert, and other early 19th-century composers, of more elaborated and sophisticated II–V–I cadences and constructions.

Chapter Four

Further Extensions of the Dominant-Tonic Relationship—VI and III

The Circle of Fifths (or Fourths)

FURTHER EXTENSIONS OF THE DOMINANT-TONIC RELATIONSHIP—VI AND III

Once the aural relationship of II to V has been understood as a logical extension of the relationship V to I, it is easy to see that the principle involves a continuity of relationships extending through dominants further removed from I. Thus VI stands in relation to II as II to V, and III stands in relation to VI as VI to II. We may perhaps call the VI and the III, in this sense, dominants twice and thrice removed from the tonic.

Like II, VI and III may occur in major as well as minor forms, and they may occur as seventh chords (major or minor) as well as simple triads. In any case, we have a chain of relationship that occurs with extraordinary frequency in traditional music, and that is completely familiar to our ears as a natural forward motion. At its greatest usual extent, it may be expressed quite simply as:

I–III–VI–II–V–I

The possibilities of variation within this formula are almost unlimited. It is one of the delights of study to discover the endless
variants of this formula in the hands of the great composers.

During the late 18th century, a normal syntactical device for
establishing the sense of key was the formula I–VI–II–V–I. It was
a favorite of Mozart, who used it countless times as a framework
for openings, as well as at other important structural points, to establish the sense of key as well as its boundaries.

Ex. 32   Mozart: Piano Sonata, K. 284 (final mov't)

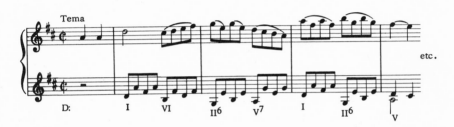

Mozart: Piano Sonata, K. 333 (opening)

The student should copy out and study similar examples in the works of Mozart and other composers, noting, as in previous studies, the modes of triads and seventh chords in the course of these progressions.

The extension of the formula to I–III–VI–II–V–I may be illustrated at its simplest in the following passage:

Ex. 33   Mozart: Piano Concerto in B♭, K. 456

This example should be studied carefully. Despite its apparent simplicity it is, as is most of Mozart, extremely subtle in its internal organization. One will note the sophisticated use of simple triads and dominant seventh chords, the weight of each of which is most carefully calculated and of course precisely right to the ear. If the music is available, the student should study the following passages of the concerto to see how the harmonic scheme contained here is developed and expanded.

Another striking example from Mozart is the following, from the four-hand Sonata in F, K. 497:

Ex. 34 Mozart: Piano Sonata, 4 Hands, K. 497 (reduced score)

The operation of the I–(III)–VI–II–V–I mechanism or formula may be likened to the setting of a spring. One may step off (so to speak) from the tonic, and proceed directly to VI or III or other relatively distant triad, but the ear senses, from experience and tradition, that this leap away from I will be followed and balanced by an orderly and regulated return to I through the normal and expected dominant relationships. In a very real sense, this mechanism is a basic means of controlling the span, time, and force of harmonic movement. It may even be suggested at this point that this mechanism may (and does) form the groundwork for larger harmonic sections within compositions of the 18th and 19th centuries, especially in the development sections of sonata forms. In other words, the simple harmonic progression (for example, VI–II–V–I) may be expanded into harmonic *sections* or key-blocs, following the same pattern.*

From this point on, the student will have to rely more and more on the resources of music available to him for study, for what must be emphasized here is not the formula itself (which is quite simple, and easily apprehended both in theory and in practice) but the infinite variety of its application. We must repeat: *the study of harmony is inseparable from a study of style.* No book, intended to serve as either a guide or a text, can begin to illustrate the wealth of ingenuity or imagination that makes the history of traditional harmonic practice. Only the music itself can do that.

What is important for the student is that he grasp the relatively simple principles that have governed the manipulation of harmonic materials and the outlines of harmonic structure. The progression of harmonic sound, or the logic of harmonic movement, by root movements of a fourth (upwards), schematically illustrated as I–(III)–VI–II–V–I, is one of these simple principles. But what variation within this simple scheme! No rules can be made or formulated for these variations. The nature of the musical plan, of the material itself, dictates which of these harmonies

* A clear example is the development section of the Beethoven Quartet, Opus 18, No. 1.

should be major, which minor; which should be a seventh chord and which should not. How long should each harmony be heard? Shall we have two measures of a harmony based on VI, and one measure of a harmony based on II? Or should these proportions be reversed? At what speed or tempo are the changes of harmony most convincingly apprehended? This, it should be noted, is a central problem for the performer.

To sum up: within the formula I–(III)-VI–II–V–I, one has at least the following variables:

a)   the mode of each harmony, major or minor (or often, with II, diminished);
b)   the use of first inversions of triads;
c)   the use or non-use of added sevenths, and the use of seventh chords in root position or inversion;
d)   the position, spacing, accent, and duration of each harmony, both absolutely and in relation to the entire progression.

Exercises:

(1)   The student may at this point study the theme of the Schubert Impromptu, Opus 142, No. 3, given in the Appendix, No. 8, noting the harmonic plan and progressions of the opening eight measures (I–II–V–I), as well as the beginning of the second eight measures on III (major) and the return to I from this more distant point.

(2)   At the keyboard (or through written exercises) the student should improvise cadence formulas in all keys on patterns (a) and (b) below.

Ex. 35

(3) The student may then proceed, as in (c), to experiment with major VI and II, and also with the addition of various simple types of non-harmonic tones. He should note when he arrives at any result that may remind him in style or sound of any given period or composer, and then try to determine the reasons.

(4) The student should then "compose" several short pieces, in free style, using the formulas I–VI–II–V–I and I–III–VI–II–V–I, in as many varied ways as possible.

THE CIRCLE OF FIFTHS (OR FOURTHS)

Once the musical fact of the I–(III)–VI–II–V–I pattern has been proved and accepted, on the basis of its use in traditional Western music, we can proceed to the completion of this series of relationships.

Two triads based on the theoretical scale steps—IV and VII— have so far not been accounted for. It is both theoretically and practically possible to carry the series back to include these. We should then have a complete schema as follows:

I–IV–VII–III–VI–II–V–I

An examination of this schema (as based on C) will reveal a curious inconsistency in the pattern: the augmented fourth between the roots of IV and VII:

C–F–B–E–A–D–G–C

Strangely enough, the ear accepts this one irregular interval without question, simply because it has been used so many thousands of times in music that it has become familiar to us. Beyond the fact that the ear accepts it, this irrational interval serves functionally as a mark of key delimitation. It is a sort of boundary. This concept requires further explanation, involving the complete traditional "circle of fifths."

The circle of fifths is based on perfect intervals (fifths or fourths), and is continuous until it returns to its point of origin. Thus:

$$C - G - D - A - E - B - F\sharp - C\sharp - (G\sharp - D\sharp - A\sharp)*$$
$$(E\flat\flat - B\flat\flat - F\flat -)C\flat - G\flat - D\flat - A\flat - E\flat - B\flat - F - C$$

*Note: keys within parentheses are theoretical.

Presented in this way, as a circle of *fifths*, each note is *followed* by its dominant. However, harmonic motion drives in the opposite direction, and it therefore seems that it would be considerably more sensible to set out the series as a circle of fourths:

$$C - F - B\flat - E\flat - A\flat - D\flat - G\flat - C\flat$$
$$C\sharp - F\sharp - B - E - A - D - G - C$$

It is entirely possible to write a series of chords or harmonies using all twelve of these tones in sequence as roots, departing from any note of the circle and returning to it.

Ex. 36

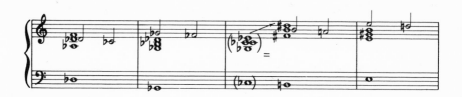

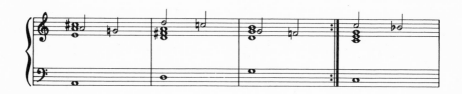

This is, in fact, the *reductio ad absurdum* of the whole process of enchained dominant harmonies. It is a *reductio ad absurdum*, because there is no boundary, no control. In a sense, there is no brake on the mechanism. One could continue this motion *ad infinitum*. It is possible, of course, to establish one of these notes as a terminus by other means, chiefly by simple insistence through extension in time, or by arbitrarily making some of the triads and sevenths minor, but by and large the entire circle of fifths remains unwieldy as a tonality-defining apparatus. It is for this reason that our ears have willingly come to accept the artificial break in the circle caused by the augmented fourth. The location of this augmented fourth may be variable.

Thus, in C, the augmented fourth is normally found between the notes F and B, the fourth and seventh (leading-tone). These are the notes that most actively demand resolution (to E and C respectively), and which are strongly activating elements of the dominant seventh chord. But by raising or lowering one of the scale tones, the augmented fourth may occur between two other notes of the series, as will be seen.

A few examples will show clearly the operation of the pattern I–IV–VII–III–VI–II–V–I:

Ex. 37 a. Mozart: Piano Sonata, K. 545

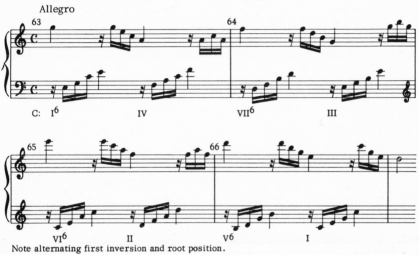

Note alternating first inversion and root position.

b. Handel: Passacaglia from Suite in G minor

c. A. Scarlatti: Toccata IV

d. A. Scarlatti: Toccata IV

In the simple and familiar example from Mozart (Ex. 37a), one should note not only the harmonic progression, but the symmetrical design of the passage: the alternation of first inversions and root positions, the parallelism of the measures melodically, and the ingenious internal melodic structure of each measure. The student should be able to appreciate the great art of such a simple passage.

Further examples in easily accessible music are:

Mozart: Piano Concerto in G major, K. 453 (first movement, measures 126–139)

Chopin: Etude, Opus 10, No. 1 (measures 35–48)

These two make an interesting comparison, as do the following:

Brahms: Ballade in G minor, Opus 118, No. 3

Chopin: Nocturne in C minor, Opus 48

The Brahms may also be compared with the Handel Passacaglia (Ex. 37b).

For an example of continuous dominant seventh chords over the entire circle, see the Tchaikovsky song, Ex. 53b, Chapter VI.

To be noted in all the above are the ways in which major and minor triads and sevenths are varied. Spacing, timing, and texture, sequential (that is, repetitive) patterns and symmetries, and other features of design should be studied carefully. The student will, without difficulty, find dozens of similar passages in music from the early 18th century to popular music and jazz of the present day. Many so-called "jazz" basses are neither more nor less than this pattern, embellished with ninths or various non-harmonic tones.

Exercise:

After carefully studying a number of examples, the student should attempt improvising or "composing" passages in various keys, using the pattern I–IV–VII–III–VI–II–V–I.

Chapter Five

The IV Chord—Its History and Function

The VII and VII⁷ Chords

THE IV CHORD—ITS HISTORY AND FUNCTION

We can see from the schemas in the preceding chapter that the IV chord is actually, in the simplest mechanism of diatonic relationships, at the greatest distance from I. In terms of the circle of fifths, it leads away from I, rather than towards it, unless the artificial break (of the augmented fourth) is made in a series in which IV is used.

Historically, the use of the IV chord in harmonic design, and especially in cadences, exhibits some curious features. By and large, one can say that the use of IV in final cadences becomes more common in the 19th century than it was in the 18th, but that it may often be understood as a substitute for the II chord when it precedes V. It may also quite logically be construed as an incomplete II⁷ chord (lacking root), just as the VII chord is often construed as a V⁷ chord lacking root. There is some degree of similarity in the way the two chords are used in traditional practice, the difference being of course that the IV is major or minor, and therefore relatively stable in sound, whereas the VII in its diminished quality is unstable. The construction of IV as an incomplete II^7 has been proposed by various theorists, but has never gained wide acceptance. It is not offered here as a statement of fact, but simply as a possibility that seems to explain a number of ambiguities in connection with the use of IV. One of the most notable of these (illustrated in the third measure from the end of the C-major Prelude from *The Well-Tempered Clavier*) is the frequency with which the missing II root (second degree of scale) shows up as a passing or other non-harmonic tone in figurations based on the IV chord. It is often difficult to decide aurally whether the note in question is "non-harmonic" or whether it actually is a conditioning factor in the harmonic structure. In this respect, the IV–II interrelation eludes generalizations.*

The so-called "plagal" cadence, that is, a direct IV–I, has an entirely different origin, and is not in reality relevant to traditional harmonic design. It is heard frequently in music of the 16th century, but it must be remembered that music of this period was not based on the kind of harmonic continuity that developed gradually through the 17th century and that is fully formulated for the first time in the works of Bach and Handel and their contemporaries. In the so-called "familiar" style of the 16th century there are, to be sure, definite chordal progressions, but they are not organized in the same way, either rhythmically or sequentially, as the chord progressions of the 18th and 19th centuries.

In traditional harmony, the IV chord, or an extended passage based on the harmony of IV, often functions in the manner of a brake, or a mechanism for slowing down harmonic action. Bach and, later, the Viennese Classicists, frequently save the sound of IV for passages towards the end of a composition, where it has an effect of tranquillity quite the reverse of dominant or II–V harmony. (This, too, is illustrated in the C-major Prelude.) In a

---

* Rameau, in his famous treatise (1722), also expressed misgivings about the subdominant, and preferred the progression II–V–I. See William J. Mitchell's interesting article, "Chord and Context in 18th-Century Theory," in *Journal of the American Musicological Society*, XVI (1963), 221–39.

sense, IV seems to exert a balance on the *opposite* side of I,* which might be illustrated in this manner:

$$(II) \quad V \quad I \quad IV$$

Many 19th-century composers who employ the pure IV (incomplete II or not) in cadential formulas lose the fine sense of balance and timing that is so notable in Bach, Handel, and Mozart, among others.

There are other indications that IV is treated as a harmony of repose, outside of the stream of dominant activity. When a flat seventh is added to the I chord (C–E–G–Bb, for example, in C), it becomes the dominant seventh of IV. This usage (V^7 of IV) is found with great frequency in traditional practice and has a markedly static effect in harmonic design. One may again refer to the Bach C-major Prelude, and to the *Wiegenlied* of Weber (Appendix, No. 5). The latter, to which we will refer again below, offers a completely unambiguous example of IV preceded by its dominant seventh, functioning as a perfect pendular balance in phrase structure to the following V^7–I.

The dominant seventh on I may of course be manipulated in other ways. It can, among other possibilities, resolve to a IV^7 and initiate a whole circle of dominant activity or it may resolve "deceptively" to II (see Chapter VII and example from Bach, Ex. 88, Chapter X). The IV^7 itself, however (like the I^7 with seventh *not* lowered), is often ambiguous both in sound and in function. Since it is a major seventh chord, the seventh often appears to be non-harmonic, often a suspension. Examples of this ambiguity may be found in the Bach C-major Prelude. Further discussion of aspects of the major seventh chord will be found in Chapter VIII.

---

* In his essay on *Harmony*, Tovey speaks of the subdominant, "whose function we should understand much more readily if we called it the anti-dominant."

The *minor* triad in IV, occurring in a major context, is found fairly often in music of the 18th century, and with increasing frequency in that of the 19th. A beautiful example is found in the *Valse Noble* of Schumann (see Appendix, No. 9). Its function remains essentially the same as that of the major IV, one of relative repose, but the "color" is very pronounced, and it becomes an "effect" that is exploited in many ways. Like the major IV, it overlaps, in a sense, the corresponding seventh chord on II, for which, in the same sense, it seems sometimes to substitute. The pure minor IV chord is, in fact, considerably less common than the II⁷ with flattened sixth scale-step, as a harmony in predominantly major passages.

Ex. 38   Bach: *St. Matthew Passion* (piano reduction)

Schubert: *Lob der Tränen*

Infrequently, a major IV chord will be heard in passages that are predominantly minor. An example will be found in the Tchaikovsky song quoted at the end of Chapter VI (Ex. 53b).

THE VII AND VII⁷ CHORDS

The VII chord in its simplest and most obvious forms is a diminished triad and must be considered, as Piston points out, a V^7 lacking the root. This is the way it is normally heard and certainly how it operates functionally. It therefore usually proceeds, just as V^7 does, to a resolution on I. Occasionally, especially in sequential passages,* VII seems to operate as a chord with a true root, and in these instances (as in the Mozart given as Ex. 37a in Chapter IV) will usually proceed to III.

VII occurs most often in its first inversion:

Ex. 39

VII may also occur as a seventh chord, in the following common forms:

Ex. 40

VII^7 with minor seventh (Ex. 40b above) is our introduction to the *diminished seventh* chord. This is, as can be seen, a seventh chord constructed entirely of superposed *minor* thirds. The sound of this chord is very unstable and ambiguous, and its movement or resolution depends almost entirely on context. It is a rootless chord; any of its possible inversions produces the same interval structure: †

---

* See Chapter VII.

† The VII^7 chord is often construed as a dominant ninth chord, lacking the root. When, in context, this chord, especially in its minor or diminished seventh form, seems clearly to be constructed on the leading-tone, this interpretation is logical and tenable, since the chord is then dominant in function and resolves usually to the tonic. The diminished seventh, however, as will be seen later, is extremely deceptive in many contexts.

Ex. 41

etc.

It will be observed that the same notes may be spelled in various ways, with the sound remaining identical. It may further be observed that there are only three sets of four notes in our twelve-note system that make diminished seventh chords of different pitch. Thus, it is evident that any one of these three possible diminished seventh chords must belong to several systems of tonality simultaneously. Because of this, their uses as pivotal points of harmonic structure are manifold.

Ex. 42

in various spellings, as above

Since the function of the diminished seventh chord will depend so largely on context, our ears readily accept a variety of movements away from it. At its simplest, it can function as a dominant. This is, however, largely a matter of style as well as of context. Bach often makes the diminished seventh a climactic sound. (See, for example, the D-major and B♭-minor Preludes of Book I of *The Well-Tempered Clavier*.) Nineteenth-century composers often use the VII⁷ as an embellishment of a V⁷, in the following manner which, incidentally, makes of the V⁷ a point of relative repose:

Ex. 43

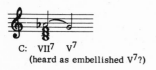

C: VII⁷ V⁷
(heard as embellished V⁷?)

This use of the diminished seventh is also illustrated in the Bach C-major Prelude, measures 22–23–24, where the structure is as follows:

Ex. 44

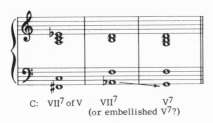

C: VII⁷ of V   VII⁷   V⁷
              (or embellished V⁷?)

Diminished seventh chords have one further notable characteristic: a succession of them, having no immediately apparent key relevance, can be enchained, and used either to provide a temporary feeling of key instability or uncertainty (which can be dramatically exploited), or simply to move rapidly to another key area. Such successions of diminished sevenths are frequent in the 19th century.

Ex. 45   C. M. von Weber: *Die Zeit*, Op. 13, No. 5

It will be noted in this example that the "sliding" effect of the diminished sevenths is temporary, and that the composer immediately reaffirms his key (A minor) in the most simple and direct way.

It may be remarked in passing at this point that one of the
curiosities of many theoretical systems is a willingness to accept
the VII⁷ with minor seventh (B–D–F–Ab) as part of the normal
harmonic vocabulary in the major mode. (It is often said to be
"borrowed" from the minor.) But at the same time, and even if
one accepts the idea of "borrowing," there has been a curious un-
willingness to extend this principle to include other common
"borrowings" that are easily observable as features of traditional
music. It is noted by a number of theorists that "borrowings" between major and minor seem to occur more frequently towards
the middle and late 19th century, but a fresh and unprejudiced
look at a dozen pages of Mozart should convince anyone that
major and minor are there already part of a single system.

We may pursue this aspect of our subject by examining other
common forms of the VII chord that are often described as "borrowed" or "auxiliary." The first of these is a major triad or dominant seventh constructed on VII:

Ex. 46

C: V of III   V⁷ of III
     (VII)

These chords function clearly as V or V⁷ of III, and may be seen
in context in the Schubert *Moment musical* (see Appendix, No.
7) and the Weber *Wiegenlied* (see Appendix, No. 5). As they
are completely functional in the key (C, in both instances), there
is no real need to regard them as anything but normal harmonies
of the same nature as the V or V⁷ of II or of V. The Weber song
is a particularly interesting example, since it very obviously does
not (in its design or its length) depart for one moment from the
key of C. We shall return to further aspects of this question in a
later chapter.

Chords of the VII are also constructed on a flattened seventh (B♭ in the key of C), which is often described as a borrowing from the descending harmonic minor. The same argument may be made here: that the concept of borrowing is in actuality unnecessary. The mixture of major and minor is a simple fact in the Classical and Romantic periods. It is especially notable in Haydn, Mozart, and Schubert, and more obviously in Chopin and Brahms. The Schubert *Moment musical* is a major-minor masterpiece, and in it the student will find the following three forms of VII:

Ex. 47

C: V of III
      VII

The triad and the seventh chord constructed on the B♭ resolve here to a flattened III (E♭–G–B♭), which may of course be described as "borrowed" from C minor. But where do minor and major begin or end in this piece?

We have seen thus far that any triad or seventh chord may be preceded in traditional harmonic construction by a harmony having a dominant relationship to it. This may be any triad or seventh chord having a root a fourth below the following chord. It is also true that VII, in its various forms, may be used in the same way, since VII is commonly heard as a dominant harmony. By introducing various forms of VII, including the diminished seventh, still further material is brought within the range of simple progressions. Thus, for example, preceding V in the key of C, we may, at this stage of study, have any of the following:

Ex. 48

C: II   II^7 V of V   V^7 of V   II$^{5♭}$ II$^7_{5♭}$ VII of V   VII^7 of V

A comparison of the Bach Chorale and the Bach Chorale Preludes (see Appendix, No. 11) will show not only how Bach uses harmonic progressions of this type to expand the scope of a composition, but also how these techniques lead eventually to a complete chromaticization of tonal harmonic progressions. Study of a number of the Chorale Preludes will demonstrate the continuity of the harmonic road from Bach to Wagner. The same principles are illustrated in the Mozart Adagio (see Appendix, No. 6). Although these works may be somewhat difficult for the student at this stage, he may begin to study them, and to make as many observations as he can. One of the techniques he will note is that of expansion by what may be called *interpolation*. At its simplest, this may be described as the elaboration of simple progressions by the interposition of leading chords or dominants. Thus, in schematic form, we might elaborate a simple progression I–II–V–I by inserting a form of V of II before II, and a form of VII of V before V:

Ex. 49

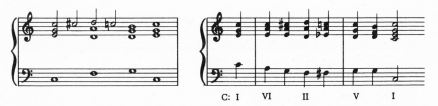

C: I   VI   II   V   I

This is a mechanism that leads directly to certain phases of 19th-century harmonic style (always remembering that these are foreshadowed in Bach and Mozart!). Considerations of style are from this point on paramount in exercises to be undertaken.

Exercise:

Write a simple piece, using *only* ordinary triads. Elaborate this piece by the interpolation of various V's, V⁷'s, VII's, and VII⁷'s. (The ambitious student may attempt to do several little pieces of this type, in approximations of various periods or styles.)

Chapter Six

The Augmented Fourth and Its Significance

The Neapolitan Sixth

The Mixed Scale

Augmented Sixth Chords

THE AUGMENTED FOURTH AND ITS SIGNIFICANCE

In Chapter IV we discussed the common occurrence of an augmented fourth in the root progression of a controlled tonal application of the circle of fifths or fourths. Over several centuries our ears have accepted this augmented fourth to such an extent that it is hardly noticed as an irregularity.

The role of the augmented fourth in tonal harmony is an extremely important one. It has been suggested previously that it sets a boundary to progressions of enchained dominant harmonies that otherwise would tend towards the infinite, or at least towards endless repetition of what we have represented figuratively as circular motion.

The root progression of the augmented fourth has one additional primary function in traditional Western harmony. Since our ears assimilate this root progression with ease (for the reasons given above and in Chapter IV), we are able to include in the concept of dominant harmony certain relations based on the augmented fourth as well as on the perfect fourth. One of the most common of these in traditional music is found in the II–V–I cadence when the root of II, preceding V, is lowered by a half step. Thus, in C, the II–V–I progression, root D, root G, root C, may also occur as root D♭, root G, root C. Similarly in other keys:

Ex. 50

Bach: *St. Matthew Passion* (piano reduction)

Mozart: Piano Concerto in G, K. 453

*See Ch. V

THE NEAPOLITAN SIXTH

It will be observed that the triad on the lowered second degree, used in progressions of this type, is *major* (Db–F–Ab), and almost invariably occurs (as is usual with the II) in its first inversion, or as a chord of the sixth.* The name given it, *Neapolitan sixth* (abbreviated as N⁶), stems from its supposedly over-frequent use in music of 17th- and 18th-century Neapolitan composers.

Examination of a number of 18th- and 19th-century works will show that harmonies (including seventh chords) built on the lowered second degree are common. It will be observed also that chords built on the lowered sixth degree are used in the same way, whether the mode of the passage is prevailingly major or minor, and are incorporated into the tonal structure without weakening the sense of key. The lowered sixth degree of course occurs normally in the minor scale, and is sometimes described as "borrowed" when it occurs in the major. (We have noted this in connection with the diminished seventh in Chapter V.) In any case, we find that relationships of this type are common:

	VI	II	V	I
in C:	A	D	G	C
	Ab	D	G	C
	Ab	Db	G	C

The root interval of the augmented fourth may occur between VI and II as well as between II and V. What becomes apparent at this stage is the possibility of still further manipulation of the augmented fourth root interval, with the consequent expansion of available harmonic and melodic material within a given key.

Limiting ourselves for the moment to the lowered second and sixth only, we can begin to see how utilization of harmonies based on these steps may lead to the eventual incorporation, within the

_____
* It also does occur, however, in root position.

concept of a single major-minor key, of chords on all twelve chromatic tones. With the lowered second and sixth alone, the student can begin to glimpse the possibilities of some interesting interrelationships. Thus, the triad or seventh chord on the lowered sixth may function as a true dominant (perfect fourth root relationship) to the triad or seventh chord on the lowered second, as it does in the following:

Ex. 51   Chopin: Nocturne, Op. 48, No. 1

This relationship may be interpreted as V^7 of N^6. In other cases, the triad on the lowered sixth may simply be construed as having the same ultimate relation to V or V^7 that the triad on the lowered II has to I. The terms N^6 of V and V of N^6 are practically interchangeable in this relationship.

What is important is that these relations, however, are real, not imagined or simply schematic. Moreover, they illustrate real extensions of the aural logic of our developed harmonic system. It is apparent that the N^6 and the N^6 of V are related in derivation and application to the adjusted or tonal circle of fifths or fourths. In Chapter IV we have seen an example of a root progression using the conventional scale steps of the major, as follows:

$$C - F - B - E - A - D - G - C$$

with the augmented fourth between IV and VII. Here, in a sense, one has the D♭–G–C (N⁶–V–I) relationship thrown back in the series. But the augmented fourth may be displaced in various ways. For example:

$$C - F - B\flat - \underline{E\flat - A} - D - G - C$$

Such complete paradigms may be found (although admittedly they are not common) in 18th- and 19th-century music.* More commonly, the displacement occurs in the following manner, as *part* of the full circle:

		I	III	VI	II	V	I
in C:		C —	E♭ —	A♭ —	D —	G —	C
or							
		C		— A♭ —	D —	G —	C

These progressions are completely familiar to the ear in music from Haydn to Brahms. The movement C to E♭ or C to A♭ (in addition to the usual C to E or C to A) adds further possibilities for root movement by thirds, which will be more fully discussed in Chapter VIII.

THE MIXED SCALE

The existence and common usage of the triads on the lowered second and sixth degrees lead us to a further consideration of a question raised in Chapter I: that of the scales—major, minor, or modal. It should be obvious that the use of a chord D♭–F–A♭ or of a chord A♭–C–E♭ will also extend the melodic material possible in C major to include the flattened notes, just as the use of the V of V (D–F♯–A) and similar dominants will allow the melodic

* See Example 53b below.

use of the sharpened notes. It can now be seen that all twelve tones (including duplicated spellings such as G♯–A♭) may occur in any given key.

The inference may be made that a scale, *as used in musical composition in any given key*, has two fixed points: tonic and dominant, and that beyond these, there is considerable variability in the other steps. This is what is meant when we point out the instability of the minor scale. But the major is, to a lesser degree, also unstable. Major and minor are less distinct and separable in musical practice than they are in elementary theory books.* Furthermore, some of the old modes, notably the Phrygian, show strong survival tendencies.† The lowered second (D♭ in the key of C) is Phrygian; the lowered sixth (A♭ in the key of C) may be construed as Aeolian or, with relation to the dominant, as Phrygian. The harmonies built on these lowered scale steps do not, of course, necessarily derive from modal harmonic practice; they have, however, as we have seen, been incorporated functionally into the practice of traditional harmony.

AUGMENTED SIXTH CHORDS

By accepting the variability of the scale, or the fact that it is a *mixed* scale, we eliminate all difficulty with what have been for so

---

* Again Busoni (*op. cit.*): "Strange, that one should feel major and minor as opposites . . . . a mere touch of the brush suffices to turn the one into the other. The passage from either to the other is easy and imperceptible; when it occurs frequently and swiftly, the two begin to shimmer and coalesce indistinguishably."

† A detailed study of the modes is a large undertaking and is not in place here. The student may be reminded, however, that the conventional notation of the Phrygian mode is that of a scale on the white notes from E to E. The half steps occur between the first and second and between the fifth and sixth degrees, while from the seventh to the tonic octave is a whole step. The Aeolian mode is set out as a scale on the white notes from A to A. The half steps here occur between the second and third and again between the fifth and sixth. From the seventh up to the tonic is again a whole tone. Some survivals of the Lydian mode (white-note scale F to F) are found in classical and romantic music. Most of the conscious "re-discovery" and exploitation of modal melody as such are 20th-century phenomena.

long termed "altered" chords. In reality, there is nothing "altered" about them; they are entirely natural elements of a single key system. This is true even of those famous *bêtes noires* of the traditional harmony course: the augmented sixth chords.

We may begin a consideration of these chords by referring to the lowered second or sixth as being a remnant of the Phrygian mode. The lowered second is clearly a supertonic with strongly reinforced tendency to move downwards to the tonic. It may be described as a leading-tone from above, and we shall refer to it in this sense as a supertonic leading-tone. Similarly, the lowered sixth has the same strong impulse to move to the dominant. We are familiar, aurally, with the strength of the drive of the leading-tone to the tonic, which is, conventionally, the distance of a semitone. But again we must remember that in earlier music, and in particular in the Dorian, Mixolydian, Phrygian, and Aeolian modes, the distance from leading-tone to tonic was a whole tone.

The importance of this historical reminder is simply to emphasize the fact that the semitone gravitates more strongly to its upper or lower neighbor than does the whole tone. The force of the dominant seventh chord is largely the result of the leading-tone's drive to the tonic and the fourth's drive to the third. We can imagine a dominant chord utilizing these two drives *plus* a strengthened drive of supertonic to tonic through lowering of the supertonic. Such a chord (Db–F–G–B) is not only theoretically possible, but is of frequent occurrence in traditional music. Its peculiarity, in our tonal system, is simply that it seldom occurs as a dominant resolving to the tonic of a key, but almost invariably as a dominant resolving to the *dominant* of the key. Thus, in C, this chord commonly occurs as follows:

Ex. 52

V   I

Verdi: *La Forza del Destino* (Act III, Intro.)

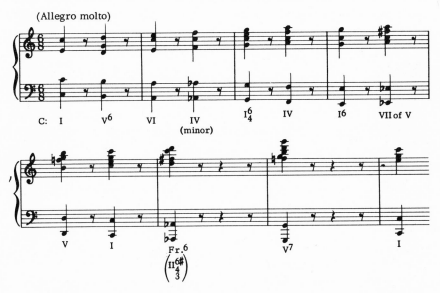

This is one of the augmented sixth chords, so denominated because of the augmented sixth interval between the Ab and F♯ (lowered sixth and raised fourth in C). There are two other common forms of augmented sixth chords, both behaving exactly as the one illustrated above (French sixth, so-called). It should be noted that all of them may resolve directly to V or indirectly to V by way of I⁶₄. The simplest augmented sixth chord consists of three notes, and is known as the Italian sixth:

Ex. 53 a. Mozart: Piano Sonata, K. 533 (1st mov't)

"Italian" and "French" sixths are found in the following:

Ex. 53 b. Tchaikovsky: *To Approaching Sleep*, Op. 27, No. 1

The so-called German sixth has as its fourth note the lowered or minor third degree of the scale (E♭ in the key of C), as follows:

Ex. 54   Mozart: Piano Sonata, K. 533 (1st mov't)

This form gives rise to certain useful ambiguities. It is, in sound, exactly like the dominant seventh chord of N^6 of V, and is often so used. Spelling the F♯ as G♭ makes this relationship clear, as in

N.B. The student is urged to examine this passage (at the end of the Exposition of the first movement) in its entirety. It is a most striking example of the embellishment of a dominant via VII (of V), VII^7 (of V), the German sixth, and the I$^6_4$, in order to confirm the establishment of a modulation and new key center.

the Chopin example above (Ex. 51). Spelling the E♭ of the German sixth as D♯ gives the chord (A♭–C–D♯–F♯) usually known as the "doubly augmented fourth." The spelling and use of the chord are determined entirely by function and context.

Like the diminished seventh, the augmented sixth may be described as a *rootless* chord, and it is easiest so to consider it. Theoreticians have differed about it. Many have professed to see in it a changed version of the subdominant or IV chord, making the root in each case F♯, and accordingly spelling the chord(s) upward as F♯–A♭ . . . (inverting the crucial interval). This does not seem to make syntactical sense, and it is suggested here that the chord is to be regarded most simply as a variety of dominant of the dominant (V of V), which is the way it seems to sound in most of its conventional applications. (Many theorists concede that the French sixth, at least, does have a II root, and that it is a dominant seventh of V, although with a diminished fifth.) * In any case, the augmented sixth chords almost invariably precede a dominant harmony, and the *two* leading-tones, usually placed at top and bottom of the note distribution, almost invariably lead outward with great force to the dominant octave, as seen in the examples above.†

Here again it should be emphasized that identification by nomenclature is the least important aspect of harmonic study. If the student hears and understands the movement of an augmented sixth chord, and sees its derivation, he may call it whatever he chooses. It is sometimes difficult to identify augmented sixth chords, especially out of context, and even more especially when the augmented sixth interval is not in the outer voices. These

---

* See Chapter VIII.

† The usual figures given for these chords, when the lowered sixth is the lowest voice, are as follows:

Italian sixth	—	6♯				
German sixth	—	6♯	—	5	—	3	or augmented six-five-three
French sixth	—	6♯	—	4	—	3	or augmented six-four-three
Doubly augmented fourth	—	6♯	—	4♯	—	3	

chords, to make matters more difficult, are occasionally misspelled, even by accomplished composers. In the following example the E♭ in the second measure should clearly be D♯.

Ex. 55 Chopin: Mazurka, Op. 67, No. 4

With the triads on the lowered second and lowered sixth degrees (Neapolitan sixth chords), with seventh chords on these degrees as well, and with the augmented sixth chords, we are now well along towards a consideration of the complete chromaticization of the scale within a given key. We may demonstrate this by indicating the available harmonic material so far discussed, and may make a twelve-tone scheme for C (major-minor-modal) along the following lines:

Ex. 56

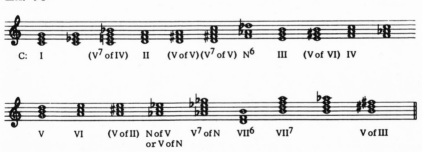

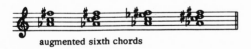

augmented sixth chords

In the key of C, it should be remembered, some of these notes (G♭ and A♯, for instance) and some of these chords will occur less frequently than others. The important thing is that they all do commonly occur. They do not necessarily imply abandonment of key (modulation), but merely its extension and elaboration. The art of harmonic construction is the maintenance of balance and relation among the possible harmonic sounds and, especially in the traditional period, the recurring reference to the tonal points of departure and arrival.

The question of "relative" major and minor may be mentioned here. It is customary to pair keys with similar signatures as related. Thus C minor (3 flats) is termed the "relative minor" of E♭ major, also 3 flats; B minor (2 sharps) the "relative minor" of D major, and vice versa. Usage gives some verisimilitude to this assumption, since "modulations," especially from minor to a "relative" major (or, harmonically, from I to III), are common in the Classical and Romantic periods. The convention must, however, be classed as one of convenience and custom, rather than as one with strong structural function. The two common notes of the fundamental triads involved (as I: C–E♭–G and III: E♭–G–B♭) make movement back and forth quite simple, as in most root movements by thirds. (See Chapter VII.) Functionally, one is inclined to agree again with Tovey, who states that "the so-called 'relative major' is one of five equally direct relations to a minor tonic and the 'relative minor' is one of five to a major tonic. The minor mode of C is not . . . A minor, but C minor." Here again, the usages of Mozart and Schubert in particular should be kept in mind.

The student may now begin to study many of the examples given in the Appendix, noting not only the harmonic vocabulary employed in various pieces, but also the over-all harmonic designs. It is important also that at this stage the student draw on his own library of music for additional material.

Exercises:

(1)   The student should improvise at the keyboard (or write out): N^6–V–I in various keys; VI–II–V–I using variable lowered degrees for VI and II, and adding sevenths at will. Augmented sixths–(I^6_4)–V–I of various types.

(2)   The student should then attempt a free "composition" using some of the formulas above.

Chapter Seven

ROOT PROGRESSION BY SECONDS

We have so far concentrated on the principal and fundamental mechanism of traditional harmonic movement: progression of dominant to tonic, or of any chord to another chord in the dominant-tonic relation, by root progression of the fourth upward or the fifth downward. There are, of course, other common progressions of structural significance. Next in importance of these, after the dominant-tonic relation, is the relation exemplified by the so-called "deceptive" cadence, or progression of V or V⁷ to VI. The sound of this progression is familiar to anyone who has listened to music. In its simplest form, in the key of C, it occurs as a progression from a triad or seventh chord with the root G to a triad or seventh chord with the root A or A♭.

Ex. 57 Haydn: Piano Sonata, B & H 33

Haydn: Piano Sonata, B & H 33

Beethoven: Piano Sonata, Op. 90 (1st mov't)

This progression elaborates the ultimate resolution of V or V⁷
to I, and is used both for harmonic variety and for extending the
length of a phrase. Thus, one frequently finds patterns of this type:

$$I-VI-II-V^7-VI-II-V^7-I$$

Measures 9–12 of the Schubert Impromptu (see Appendix, No. 8)
illustrate this formula. By resolving V or V⁷ to VI instead of to I,
the harmonic motion can be retraced and the musical phrase extended.

Further extension of this harmonic mechanism is obviously possible. If the ear accepts, through custom and convention, the root
movement of the second upward from V to VI, it will accept with
equal ease a movement from IV to V, from II or II⁷ to III, or most
analogous progressions. Such progressions will be used for expressive purposes, for variety, and for extending the length or scope of
a phrase. The magnificent opening of the slow movement of the
Third Piano Concerto of Beethoven shows many of these. (See Appendix, No. 11.) This passage requires careful study; for the moment, the student should observe the effectiveness of the dominant
seventh on B resolving to C♯ (measure 2), the dominant seventh
on D resolving to E (measures 9–10), the movement from the root
F♯ upward to root G♯ in measures 3–4, and from root B to root
C♮ in measures 10–11. The C♮ root returning to the B root is a
so-called Phrygian cadence, the relationship of which to the N⁶
should be clearly apparent.

It will be found, in the practice of traditional harmony, that root
movements of seconds do not often appear successively. When two
or more root progressions of seconds are heard, it is almost certain
that they will be followed by a strongly reemphasized succession of
dominant-tonic harmonies. The reason for this is implicit in the
nature of our harmonic language and its natural forward thrust.
Root movement by seconds is commonly found in modal harmony,

as in the familiar style of the 16th century, but in tonal harmony it tends in a comparatively short time to dissipate the sense of gravitational force that is the essence of tonal organization.

THE FIRST INVERSION SERIES

Root progressions by whole or half step downward occur in traditional harmony, but are generally heard as weak progressions, or intermediary steps in a larger scheme. Like progressions of the second upward, they seldom occur successively, and for the same reasons. In successive stepwise root progressions there is, aside from the impression of tonal weakness, a difficulty in avoiding parallelisms in the voices. This difficulty is almost always resolved by alternating root positions and first inversions. For continued movement by stepwise root progressions, first inversions are used almost exclusively. The first inversion series is rather a special device in traditional music:

Ex. 58   Mozart: Piano Sonata, K. 533

Beethoven: Piano Concerto No. 4 (1st mov't)

It will be seen that these successions of first inversion triads are nothing more than scale passages in parallel voices rather than in single notes. Their harmonic significance is to emphasize key by the melodic means of the scale rather than by the harmonic connections of the successive sixth chords. It will be noted that in almost all cases where such first inversion series occur, a strong II–V–I follows to fix the center of harmonic gravity. The first inversion series can be used as a simple mechanism for changing the harmonic center or key, as it can be interrupted at any step and diverted into a cadential formula.

SEQUENCES

The first inversion series lends itself easily to sequential formulas, in which a melodic or figural pattern is repeated at various step levels. This device is somewhat overworked at times in Handel, as well as in Corelli and Vivaldi:

Ex. 59   Corelli: Concerto Grosso No. 9

Handel: Suite No. 13, Allemande

Handel: Suite No. 1, Gigue

Sequences of this sort, involving melodic repetition, but with a more functional harmonic basis, are of course a characteristic of Classical and Romantic music. The most common harmonic sequences usually involve dominant-tonic relationships as well as stepwise ones. Some of the less common stepwise progressions (III to IV, or VI to VII, for example) occur often enough in sequences of this type. In the following example, one should note particularly the stepwise descending movement of the bass, which is accomplished by the alternation of root position and first inversion triads.

Ex. 60   Mozart: Sonata for Two Pianos, K. 448 (last mov't)

This example is characteristic of the Classical style in general and of Mozart in particular in its perfect balance and completeness. The sequence leads back to the tonic from which it starts, and thence proceeds to the usual II–V–I cadence, repeated for emphasis. (From the standpoint of composition, or the utilization of harmonic material, it is important to note how sequences are terminated; they are sometimes easier to begin than to end convincingly.) The symmetry of the sequence above is perfect, and a schematization of its harmonic plan will demonstrate the elements of a highly sophisticated design:

$$\underline{\text{I}} - \text{V} \mid \underline{\text{VI}} - \text{III} \mid \underline{\text{IV}} - \text{I} \mid \underline{\text{II}} - \text{V} - \text{I} \text{ etc.}$$

step   half-step   step

There is here a succession of movements to triads in dominant relationship (I–V, VI–III, IV–I) with each "dominant" resolving "deceptively" upward by step or half-step. The parallelism of the relationships is obvious: I is to V as VI is to III and as IV is to I; equally, V is to VI as III is to IV and I is to II. With the third section of the sequence, the I chord is reached, at which point it must be re-established as the effective tonic or stopping point. This is accomplished by proceeding, in continued parallelism, from I to II (continuing the sequence V–VI and III–IV) but using II, with the suggestion of a preceding VI, as a pivotal V of V leading to V and I.

One other relation of interest is found in the sequence, which is constructed quite clearly of two-measure elements. In each two-measure unit, a harmonic movement of descending thirds (I–VI–IV–II) will be discovered. We shall consider this relation directly.

All circle of fifths (or fourths) progressions may be considered harmonic sequences. Such sequences may be made explicit by alternations of regular chordal patterns or figurations, as, for example, the alternation of sevenths and simple triads, or of arpeggiated and block chords. If one arranges the series in rhythmic units of two, one will find that the effect of stepwise root progression is obtained. Thus:

$$I - IV - VII - III - VI - II - V - I$$
$$\quad\ F \qquad\quad E \qquad\quad D \qquad\quad C$$
$$C \qquad\quad B \qquad\quad A \qquad\quad G$$

The arrangement is, in effect, a stepwise root progression with interpolated dominants.* A similar technique may be used for stepwise ascending progressions:

$$I - V \text{ of } II - II - V \text{ of } III - III \text{ etc.}$$
$$\text{Roots: } C \qquad\qquad D \qquad\qquad\quad E$$
$$\qquad\qquad\ A \qquad\qquad\ B$$

* The reader is reminded that in our tradition the irrational interval of the augmented fourth (F—B) is accepted by the ear in progressions of this type, even though there is no acoustical or theoretical justification for it.

It is, in fact, in very much this way that most stepwise root progressions appear in traditional practice. The technique is used with great frequency not only in sequences of all types, but in modulatory passages and elsewhere. The important conclusion here is not so much that a form of dominant harmony may be placed before almost any chord in a progression, but that such interpolation is a normal procedure in Classical and Romantic music. It is, in fact, the technique that facilitates the widest variety of harmonic movement and change. The application of the technique becomes more elaborated (in terms of length and extension) as harmonic styles evolve through the 18th and 19th centuries. The "difficulties" of late 19th-century chromatic harmony, as for example in Wagner, are in large part the elaborations of what are in essence simple processes of this type.

In its essentials, the technique, whether found in sequences or in other passages, is the movement from one root to another by means of an intervening harmony. Structurally, the intervening harmony may have less weight (though not necessarily) than the harmonies it connects. Our hearing (and therefore our analysis) takes account of the factors of weight and emphasis. The logic of harmonic connection must be understood aurally; it is the sole purpose of "analysis" to assist aural understanding, and perhaps to assist the performer in facilitating that understanding through his own clarity of harmonic perception in terms of phrase, weight, balance, and timing.

In phrases that are of perfect harmonic symmetry and balance, the ear perceives readily the extended movement and direction. Even the inexperienced listener will hear, for example, the fundamental movement from II to I at the beginning of the middle section of the Mozart Sonatina (see Appendix, No. 4) where the complete sequential progression is:

$$N^6 \text{ of } II - V \text{ of } II - II$$
$$N^6 \text{ (of } I) - V \text{ (of } I) - I$$

ROOT PROGRESSION BY THIRDS

Root movement up or down by thirds does not occur very frequently in music before Haydn, but it is found with increasing frequency from the late 18th century through the 19th, as the syntax of harmonic relation becomes more complex through building on its already established vocabulary, or as departures from the simpler forms of progression become easier for the ear to assimilate in the framework of normal expectation. Both Beethoven and Schubert made much of root movement by thirds. Harmonic successions built on such root movements now sound smooth and logical to our ears by reason of their constant use. They originally had (and to some extent still do have) the effect of surprise and variety; but they are considerably less novel, though not necessarily less effective, to our ears than they must have been to ears of the early 19th century.

(It should be noted here that a root movement of a third down is the same as that of a sixth up, and vice versa, with major third the equivalent of minor sixth, and minor third the equivalent of major sixth. Thus a progression from root C to root A or Ab will be construed as a third progression, even though the bass may actually move upwards.)

The most common and familiar root movement of a third is that from I to VI, and it is from this progression that further movement by thirds may be derived. The interpolation of a IV chord in the common I–VI–II–V–I progressions produces a series I–VI–IV–II–V–I as in the Mozart above (Ex. 60). It is to be noted that the triads in this series overlap, two notes of each pair (I–VI, VI–IV, IV–II) being held in common. This makes the transition from one to the next both simple and grateful:

Ex. 61 Brahms (See below, Ex. 63)

C: I   VI   IV   II   G#: I   VI   IV   II   VII   V   I

Ex. 62   Bach: Chorale, *Der Tag, der ist so freudenreich*, B & H, 158

An interesting example of the handling of downward third progressions is provided by Brahms:

Ex. 63   Brahms: Intermezzo, Op. 116, No. 6

Here we have first a series I–VI–IV–V–I, followed by an expansion to the complete cycle: I–VI–IV–II–VII–V–I.

In isolated instances of movement from VI to IV, the IV chord at times seems to be an unexpected substitute for II:

Ex. 64   Schubert: *Valses nobles*, Op. 77

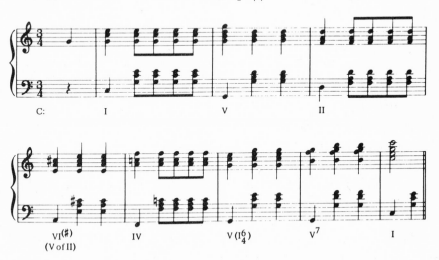

The effect of the F major triad following the A major is still fresh and surprising.

Root movements by thirds may involve both major and minor thirds and major and minor triads. The progression from I to a triad on the lowered sixth (C to A♭) is common. Liszt and later composers occasionally employed a series of major thirds in the fashion C–A♭|G♯–E–C, but this is rather unstable tonally. It is found (in Liszt and Hugo Wolf) also in an upward direction.

Root progressions of ascending thirds are somewhat less common, but are to be found. The movement from I to III is common, and usually heard as the beginning of a series I–III–VI–II, etc. But III may form a pivot to V as well. The most effective application of the upper third relation is found not in single chord relations, but on a larger scale in 19th-century music. Beethoven frequently uses III as a contrasting tonal *area*, as for example in the *Waldstein Sonata* (C major, with second subject in E major) or in the Fourth Piano Concerto, where the key-areas of G and B are strikingly juxtaposed. These scores should be studied by the advanced student.

With the exception of the downward progression of thirds (I–VI–IV–II . . .), which is easy to handle even in a limited scope, and which occurs frequently in traditional practice, progressions by thirds must be employed with care. Over-use, or over-extension, tends to weaken a sense of harmonic direction or center, and a succession of root movements by thirds must eventually be brought back into tonal control and focus by a reversion to dominant-tonic progressions. A study of the Schubert *Moment musical* (see Appendix, No. 7) is interesting in this respect. In the section given, an almost teasing use is made of the relation between I and III, and the ambiguity inherent in the two common notes of the triad is delightfully exploited. This is the sort of thing that both Schubert and Beethoven did with immense skill. Manipulation of this sort (even on so small a scale as the Schubert piece in question) is of course in the higher regions of the art of composition, rather than in that of the harmony exercise. Nevertheless, it is only through attempting to manipulate the materials himself that the student comes to perceive the artistic mastery in even the smallest and simplest pieces of the greatest composers.

AMBIGUITY AND CONSIDERATIONS OF TIME

It must be clear that the central problem, not only in the handling of ambiguous or subtle harmonic relationships but in any harmonic progressions whatsoever, is one involving *time:* the absolute time in which the unstable or ambiguous movement evolves, and the relative time, or time elapsing in relation to the fixed or tonally centered passages. The problem is clearly illustrated in the page of Schubert. One must note first the absolute clarity of the opening phrase in C: three measures of a pure and unmistakable C-major triad, followed by one measure of dominant-tonic. This is

so firmly established that the wonderful next four measures, and
the whole next phrase, fall into place with the utmost clarity in
their relation to C. In measure 16 we come to rest on a B-major
triad, V of III. Then follows perhaps the most important structural touch in the piece: one measure of silence! then, *piano*, two
measures with only the notes E and G. Are these the resolution
of the V of III, E–G–B? Or is the third note to be C? The two
measures of ambiguity prepare us for the C in measure 20, and we
are reassured of the tonal center by six clear measures of C major.
The marvelous closing is a masterpiece of subtlety. (It is, incidentally, an inversion of measures 5–8.) Opening with a C-minor
triad, it proceeds to a harmonic sequence G–C, Bb–Eb, D–G,
G–C. The bass here outlines the chords G–Bb–D–G and C–Eb–
G–C. It nevertheless seems to depart oddly from C major. But
the movement in even eighth notes stops when the dominant
seventh on G is reached. Here we have, marked *forte-piano*, the
crucial sound held for the length of a dotted quarter. It is both
longer and louder than the harmonies preceding it, and it is this
that satisfies our ears that it is, in fact, the important dominant
that returns us conclusively to the tonic C.

Considerations such as these must be borne in mind in any attempt at serious harmonic analysis, and *a fortiori*, in any attempt to
come to grips with the structure and nature of music that is based on
harmonic procedures. It is by no means enough to identify chords
or chordal sounds. Length, speed, proportion, and loudness of
harmonic sounds all must be considered. It is demonstrably true
that any student can learn to put together a "correct," and perhaps
even a complex, progression. But not every student succeeds in
composing, which is a different matter. Composition can be
learned only from composers; that is, by studying their music.
What is important is to learn what to study in this music.

The student who wishes to learn from Bach or Mozart or
Beethoven or Schubert will observe as well as he can, on every
page he studies, just such elements, simple or subtle, as we have

attempted to indicate in the page of the *Moment musical*. It should be apparent at this point that chord progression offers almost limitless possibilities; one can go from almost any triad to almost any other. Some relation between any pair of triads or seventh chords can be found theoretically, and can be managed in practice. But coherence depends on more than isolated relation: relation in grammar or syntax must be continuous, at least from a traditional point of view. The fundamental consideration in our musical tradition is that of tonality or unity of key. A key is more than the relation of its principal triads: it is their extension in time, and the relation of all the parts to a whole. One can make almost any sort of excursion or digression, in a harmonic sense—in other words, one can go very far from the point of departure—but one must always have the return to that point in mind. This return is calculated not in pitch manipulation so much as it is in actual measurable time.* (It is possible to return from anywhere to a tonic in three or four chords, but if one were in F♯ minor for ten minutes, a return to C major in ten seconds would hardly be convincing.) More will be said on this point when the subject of modulation is discussed.

Exercises:

(1) The student should do certain exercises schematically, principally for the purpose of satisfying his own ear. It is recommended that the following be done as simply as possible (all in various keys):

1) I–V–I–V–VI–II–V–I
2) I–V–I–VI–IV–II–V–I
3) I–V–I–II–III–VI–II–V–VI–II–V–I
4) I–V–I–VI–V–IV–II–V–I
5) I–V–I–VI♭ and back to I by any method.

(2) If the student is able to play the piano, he should then take any or all of these formulas and attempt to improvise coherent passages in various figurations.

---

* In this connection, see the concluding page of the *Tarantella* of Liszt, reprinted in the Appendix.

Chapter Eight

More on Seventh Chords

Equivocal and Unequivocal Chords

The Diminished Seventh

Ninth, Eleventh, and Thirteenth Chords

Summary

MORE ON SEVENTH CHORDS

We have seen in previous chapters that seventh chords establish in our ears an expectation of resolution, that they are, in other words, *chords of motion* implying an extension of sound in time. They demand to be followed by another sound which, in the simplest context, will be a static sound of rest or of termination.

We have also seen, however, that seventh chords may be followed by other seventh chords, and that the motion, or sense of motion, may be prolonged considerably before a point of absolute or relative rest is reached. We have noted, moreover, that it is possible to construct seventh chords other than the dominant seventh or the II^7; that it is possible, in fact, to construct seventh chords on any note and to integrate them within a tonality or key. The student will have observed that the construction of these seventh chords varies; that is, the intervals of which they are composed, although all are major or minor thirds, vary in order of superposition. Thus, the dominant seventh is seen to consist, reading from the root upwards, of a major third, a minor third, and another

minor third (G–B–D–F). The most common seventh chords built
on the second degree of the scale consist of a minor third, a major
third, and a minor third (D–F–A–C), or a minor third, minor
third, and major third (D–F–A♭–C).

In all, we have these principal types of seventh chords:

Intervals (reading up):

a) Major-minor-minor   common dominant seventh

b) Minor-major-minor   II⁷, III⁷, and VI⁷ (in major), sometimes called a minor seventh chord

c) Minor-minor-major   VII⁷ (major), II⁷ (minor), etc., sometimes called "half-diminished" (al-
though this terminology is misleading)

d) Minor-minor-minor   VII⁷ (with flat), diminished seventh
chord

e) Major-minor-major   I⁷, IV⁷ (major); VI⁷ (minor), sometimes called a "major" seventh chord

Ex. 65

The five types of seventh chords illustrated above are the most
common ones in traditional harmony. There are other types, not
frequently encountered in the 18th century, which become more
usual in the 19th. These include the dominant seventh with raised
fifth:

Ex. 66   Chopin   Schumann

and the dominant seventh with lowered fifth. This chord is described in most theoretical works as having an independent existence, but it is often confused with the so-called French augmented sixth chord, from which, in most cases, it is actually indistinguishable.* In the following, for example, one nomenclature is as good as the other:

Ex. 67   Schumann

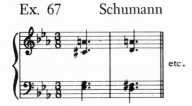

etc.

EQUIVOCAL AND UNEQUIVOCAL CHORDS

The nomenclature or terminology of many of the seventh chords, other than the dominant seventh, tends to be confusing. There is, in fact, no standard descriptive nomenclature, and musically speaking this is perhaps just as well. For the sevenths should be classified not only by how they may sound in isolation, or in the abstract, but more importantly by how they function in a given context. Further, the subjective sense of hearing will often make the same notes appear to have different sounds in different contexts. In late 19th-century music it is often futile to attempt to "analyze" passages by giving names to the many types of sevenths (or augmented sixths, or other more or less complex vertical configurations), for the simple reason that they are not isolated sounds of sharply defined identity. The configurations, although logically connected in terms of a consistent harmony, are reached for the most part by linear movement. They are, in a sense, "vertically" fluid and equivocal or ambiguous. (This is discussed further in Chapter X.)

* It is usually described as an augmented sixth chord when the flattened fifth is in the bass.

In the traditional harmony of the 18th and early 19th centuries, the first three (Exx. 65a, b, c above) of the seventh chords above are normally used *unequivocally:* that is, they are heard as basic harmonic entities or structural units, and each of them tends strongly to resolve to a harmony on a new root—most often, as we have seen, a root a fourth or a second higher. (The dominant seventh with raised fifth is also almost always used unequivocally; it is syntactically not different from the usual dominant seventh, but the raised fifth gives added impetus to a resolution on the major third.)

The term "unequivocal," as used here, requires further explanation. It has been suggested that the use of the term implies a definite aural identification of a structural harmonic sound. Thus, when Bach comes to rest on a diminished seventh chord, as in the following example:

Ex. 68   Bach: Prelude in B♭ minor, *Well-Tempered Clavier,*
       Book I

there can be no doubt that this is indeed a chordal unit, and that no non-harmonic tones are involved. Similarly, when Beethoven uses the dominant seventh, as here:

Ex. 69   Beethoven: Symphony No. 1

or Mozart uses a II⁷ in a cadence, as:

Ex. 70 Mozart: Piano Concerto in G major, K. 453 (finale)

we cannot hesitate in our identification and understanding of the sound.

This is important precisely because *all* of the seventh chords, and especially the "major" seventh and the diminished seventh, can be used equivocally, and often cannot be identified until they are no longer heard. In other words, their nature, as well as their function, cannot be defined except in terms of what follows them. The diminished seventh chord, ordinarily used with great clarity by Bach (as in Ex. 68 above), becomes in the 19th century a floating sound (as in *Tristan*), which keeps the ear in constant suspense.

With the major seventh, from its earliest appearances, the seventh seems to occur most frequently not as a true chord tone, but as an auxiliary tone or suspended dissonance. In such instances, we are justified in saying that although the sound of a seventh chord is momentarily apprehended, the sense of a seventh chord as a structural element is lacking. An example may be noted in measure 8 of the Bach Prelude in C major (see Appendix, No. 1). This is an artful ambiguity, and the major seventh is often used in just this way. The major seventh typically is found as involving either an appoggiatura or a suspension:

Ex. 71

We expect all seventh chords to resolve to chords on another root, and in traditional harmony all true seventh chords eventually

do so. We further expect that the seventh itself will in almost all
cases resolve downwards. But how and when are matters of style,
not of grammar or syntax. Delay or diversion in the resolution becomes increasingly characteristic of 19th-century style. We must
remember that our sense of hearing, and our recognition of logic
in harmonic progressions, has developed historically. The history
of the seventh chords is instructive. In the 16th century, the interval of the seventh, defined and understood as a dissonance, could
not be introduced without preparation. The introduction of the
seventh, whether in two-part writing or in fuller textures, was
normally by means of the suspension: the carrying over of one note
that became dissonant as the other voices moved, usually by step.
Thus:

Ex. 72

The seventh introduced in this way is termed "prepared." It is
usually stated that Monteverdi was the first to use an unprepared
seventh chord. In any case, it is true that the unprepared seventh
appears in the early 17th century as a new and revolutionary sound,
and that its introduction gave impetus to the development of
traditional harmony. Although traditional harmony no longer de-
manded that the seventh be prepared, it did retain the convention
that it had to be resolved as in previous centuries. With the major
seventh chord, preparation also remained usual for most of the
Classical period. The voice relations in Mozart, however, are occasionally of the following order:

Ex. 73   Mozart: Concerto in G major, K. 453

(first movement,

meas. 128–130)

THE DIMINISHED SEVENTH

The diminished seventh chord differs from all other sevenths in that it does not, except by context, have a root. Each of its members is equal (one can say that it is, both figuratively and literally, equi-vocal); none has a greater tendency towards resolution than any other. The diminished seventh can be constructed on any pitch, in any key, and can resolve in a multitude of ways, each of which can be made to seem natural and logical. With Bach, as in Example 68 cited above, the diminished seventh is usually encountered in its simplest tonal context, most often as a chord recognizably built on a seventh degree or leading-tone. It hence functions as a dominant, either of the tonic chord itself or of a closely related tonal triad. But as the sound of the diminished seventh becomes historically more familiar, its use becomes more frequent and more casual, and its potential as a pivot or as a delaying chord is further explored by each succeeding generation of composers. Diminished sevenths appear at all points, often through contractions of other sevenths, and they do not always appear as dominant in function. Following are some typical progressions:

Ex. 74

Diminished seventh may also follow diminished seventh, with a complete absence of any dominant function or tonal direction, as in the Chopin example quoted in the Appendix, No. 16. With Wagner, especially in *Tristan*, protracted use of diminished seventh and augmented sixth chords results in what amounts to a suspension of tonality for fairly long stretches. The matter of perceiving the logic of such progressions is often complicated by the question of spelling. With our equal temperament, there are, as has been noted previously, only three possible pitch-levels of the diminished seventh chord. These can, however, be spelled in

twelve different ways, as for example the diminished seventh
F♯–A–C–E♭, which contains the same notes as the diminished
sevenths D♯–F♯–A–C, A–C–E♭–G♭, and C–E♭–G♭–B♭♭. Even the
masters are not always orthographically precise in their uses of
these sounds. Theoretically, at least, the chords D♯–F♯–A–C and
E♭–G♭–A–C, although containing the same notes, in the same dis-
position, should not proceed in the same manner.

It is, however, possible to have it both ways: to arrive at a diminished seventh quite correctly in one spelling, and to leave it,
just as correctly, in another. This technique clearly allows for
sudden and surprising changes of tonal orientation. The governing
principle in all such cases is a simple one. Our ears have been con-
ditioned to expect sharpened tones to continue to move in an
upward direction. (Thus in C, when we hear an F♯, we expect it
to go on to G, and not back to F♮.) Conversely, we expect flattened tones to continue to move downward. In most cases, this is
what does happen. What is termed chromatic harmony is in essence nothing more than the interpolation of sharpened and
flattened tones in conventional progressions. The result is often an
elongation that becomes difficult to follow. From the standpoint
of analysis, one must always keep in mind that chords of odd configuration do not occur in isolation. They cannot always be identified; certainly they cannot be taken out of context and expected to
reveal any meaning.

Our hearing of these sounds is at least in part subjective.
Whereas in analyzing with a score we can see a given spelling,
correct or not, we cannot always know, through hearing, especially
on an instrument such as the piano, if an F♯ or a G♭ is the intended tone. We are therefore all the more dependent on our
ability to recollect and to anticipate: to make a progression coherent as it evolves in time. The many techniques and devices of
suspension, anticipation, delay, diversion, or embellishment, especially as used in the 19th century, are simply ways of extending
harmonic sound in time, of forcing the ear to more sustained effort,
and through the ear, of forcing the mind to synthesize. And again it

must be emphasized that both relative time (proportion) and absolute time (speed and duration) are involved. If motion is sufficiently fast, in any given passage, then all non-harmonic tones may be heard as simple embroidery, of no structural significance. The same may be true of conglomerate sounds such as the diminished seventh, which may be heard as nothing more than a fleeting connective sound. But on the other hand, the same notes, at slower speeds, may suggest relationships of a far more complex nature.

Perhaps the point can be made clearer by referring again to the $^6_4$ chord. It is obvious that if one takes this configuration out of context, one is tempted to identify it, very much as one would identify a laboratory specimen. If one does this, with G–C–E, for example, one can describe it as a C-major triad with the fifth in the lowest voice. But this chord cannot exist in isolation, or out of context, and we can easily verify that in context it is usually an appoggiatura to the chord G–B–D. In traditional harmony, the I$^6_4$ is in almost all cases a V chord approached by embellishment from above; the $^6_4$ thus is seen to represent a function of motion, just as does the seventh chord, and in the same sense of movement from dissonance (relative) to consonance.

NINTH, ELEVENTH, AND THIRTEENTH CHORDS

What is true of the $^6_4$ is also true of some chords that appear to be seventh chords, and also of most so-called ninth chords. We may, for example, have a chord of the following type:

Ex. 75

which appears to be a reasonable seventh chord configuration (major, major, and minor thirds), but which almost invariably proves to be, in context, a simple triad with two non-harmonic tones. The D♯ and F♯ will usually move upward to E and G, and the true structural character of the chord will be revealed as a

minor triad on E. False seventh chords of this and similar types
occur in 18th-century music, but become much more common in
the 19th century.

Many ninth chords are "false" in this sense, and, *a fortiori*, so
are almost all configurations termed chords of the eleventh or thirteenth. All are theoretically possible, but instances of unequivocal
use are rare before the late Romantic period, and even in Chopin
and Wagner many ninths, and certainly most elevenths, are du-
bious.

The ninth chord is formed by adding still another third to a
seventh chord; the eleventh and thirteenth by superimposing still
more thirds. To have these chords complete, textures of five, six,
or seven voices are required. The eleventh and thirteenth are almost never found complete before the beginning of the 20th
century; when they occur in incomplete form, they almost always
are the result of passing voice movements that resolve into simpler
harmony. (See excerpt from Chopin C-minor Nocturne, Appendix
No. 17.)

Major and minor dominant ninths, however, appear occasionally
in simple and unambiguous form, as here:

Ex. 76   Schubert: *Atzenbrucker Deutsche* No. 3

Schubert: *Valses nobles,* Op. 77

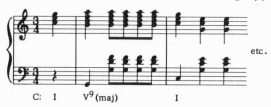

The minor dominant ninth is used with immense effect by Beethoven in the *Waldstein Sonata*:

Ex. 77 Beethoven: Piano Sonata in C major (*Waldstein*),
    Op. 53 (3rd mov't)

These G's are pedal points.

To be particularly noted here is the dynamic balance of the whole passage, with its wonderful spacing and timing, and its powerful use of the diminished sevenths. The simple dominant seventh at the close is by contrast a sound of repose, a perfect preparation for the burst of clear C major that follows to conclude the movement.

The sound of the dominant *with* ninth is certainly heard often enough in 19th-century music. There are, as in the examples above, instances of clear and unequivocal complete ninth chords. But for the most part, the ninth turns out to be an auxiliary tone (accented upper neighbor, appoggiatura, or passing tone), resolving down to the dominant root (A or Ab to G) and establishing itself as a simple seventh chord. The most significant fact about the ninth, as it occurs in 19th-century music, is that it makes of the seventh chord, in context, a point of relative repose. Nothing more clearly indicates the shifting nature of our definition of sounds in terms of tradition and style.

The following is typical of the appoggiatura ninth, eleventh, and thirteenth:

Ex. 78 C. M. von Weber: Piano Sonata, Op. 24 (1st mov't)

We hear this type of sound constantly in Mendelssohn, Schumann, and other composers of the first half of the 19th century.

The following is another type of ambiguous ninth, which eventually is heard as falling into a dominant seventh:

Ex. 79   Tchaikovsky: Symphony No. 6

Still another characteristic cadential formula of the 19th century is the following:

Ex. 80

This chord should not be identified as a ninth chord with root E (E–G–B–D–F), which would make little sense. The E is a non-harmonic tone with an ordinary dominant seventh chord. It is true that we often hear this sound proceeding to a tonic without resolution to D, as in the following:

Ex. 81

but this is best understood as a form of *elision,* a subject to be discussed in a later chapter.

SUMMARY

We have now discussed most of the common chordal configurations found in the music of the 18th and 19th centuries. It will be obvious to the student who has examined any music of this period that harmonic analysis is not always simple, and that structural logic is not always crystal clear. One of the more obvious difficulties in analyzing (and one must remember that analysis is useful only as it helps one to hear) is that of determining, especially in 19th-century music, just which notes are actually chord-tones, and which may be passing tones, appoggiaturas, neighboring notes, or other non-harmonic tones resolving into simpler forms of triads or sevenths. Time and motion must always be considered; a chord cannot be isolated and examined any more than a verb in a sentence can be, if one does not have any idea of the subject or object. It may be "understood" in a certain sense, but it does not have any meaning beyond its own identification as a part of speech or as the indication of an undefined action.

Time and motion are both absolute and relative in musical composition. Tovey brilliantly points out that the harmonic materials employed by composers from Bach to Wagner do not really differ in basic logic or structure. The difference is "the range over which the listener must depend on his memory." Or again, "Wagner's sense of key is exactly the same as Beethoven's; but it has hours in which to exercise itself, whereas Beethoven's designs seldom stretch without break over fifteen minutes, and always show their purport within five . . ."*

We see this in simple instances, the delayed resolution of a seventh chord, the prolonged non-harmonic tone, the extension of a passage through the circle of fifths, and so on. These delays and extensions become more involved as musical tradition and history builds on itself. The sound that appears strange or incomprehensible to one generation seems a matter of course to the next. The greatest composers are usually the most subtle. There is a world of

* Tovey, "Harmony," in The Forms of Music.

difference in making auditory sense between a simple tonic-dominant A–B–A piece (such as the Leopold Mozart Polonaise in the Appendix, No. 2), and such a masterpiece of subtle art as the Adagio, K. 594 (see Appendix, No. 6) by Leopold's son. One who understands this Adagio aurally is well along towards an understanding of Wagner's harmony. Wagner's technique, however complex it appears at times, is directly descended from the technique used by Mozart in works such as this Adagio and in the E♭ Quartet, K. 428. The major difference is one of time span. Wagner is essentially traditional in his harmonic syntax, but his resolutions of sevenths or ninths or augmented sixth chords are often tantalizing or deceptive or simply so long spun-out that we have difficulty in following the chain of sound. Tovey states that "the most distinctive feature of Wagner's harmony is his use of long auxiliary notes in such a way as to suggest immensely remote keys, which vanish with the resolution." It must be noted, however, that the remote keys not infrequently are reached. One of Wagner's favorite devices (used of course by others as well) is schematically simple enough: while the dissonant element of a complex resolves, other voices also change. Thus, while the normal expectation of the ear is in the one instance satisfied (by resolution), it is at the same time challenged because the ground has shifted. The ear must quickly re-orient itself. Technical mannerisms such as these made much of Wagner's music seem radical and confusing when it was first heard; it must be remembered that even Berlioz was unable to make sense of the *Tristan* Prelude.

What sometimes seems confusing in Chopin too is almost always found to have a direct logic based on simple harmonic progression. Chopin, perhaps more than any other 19th-century composer, is directly and profoundly Mozartean in his harmonic thought, although he did not have Mozart's power or range. And yet Chopin in many passages anticipates Wagner. The passage from the C-minor Mazurka, Opus 56, No. 3 (analyzed in the Appendix, No. 16), is a representative example. Before attempting either aural or visual analysis of complex Wagnerian passages, the student should examine many pages of Chopin (and also of late Mozart), in which "Wagnerian" harmonic characteristics will be found, but without the great extension in time that still makes the synthesis of many passages of Wagner difficult.

Exercise:

The student should take any of the exercises or "compositions" that he has done up to this point, and make interpolated connections by moving voices by half steps, one or two voices at a time. A further experiment may be made by interpolating a number of diminished seventh chords in an already written exercise.

Part Two

Chapter Nine

Tonality and Time-Span

Modulation and Sub-division

Key "Area"

Harmonic Plan

Analysis of the Clementi G-major Sonatina,
Opus 36, No. 2

TONALITY AND TIME-SPAN

At the conclusion of Part I, the time-span involved in harmony was briefly discussed. It is from this point that one must begin a consideration of the larger forms of harmonic organization, which may in turn be defined as a consideration of the *relatedness* of harmonies over longer spans. This is, in essence, the entire meaning of tonality.

Tonality is a central principle in music of the period with which we are concerned, and there can be little question that it is both a technical and an esthetic preoccupation of composers from the mid-17th century to the end of the 19th. It is, as we have suggested in the Introduction, a fundamental element of unity in traditional Western music, which is based on harmonic continuity as its chief mechanism of extension and development. Tonality may be regarded as the integration of harmonic units, from single chords to harmonic phrases and larger sections, within a scheme of any dimension. The scope of a tonal scheme, including the "area" of

any given key, or the extent of exploration and exploitation of relationships within it, may vary widely. Tonality, or a tonal scheme,
may in the smallest sense (as in the Leopold Mozart Polonaise,
Appendix, No. 2) be expressed by no more than three triads (two
of which must obviously be tonic and dominant) so disposed as to
produce a complete and coherent form. A tonal scheme at its
largest, as for example in Beethoven's Ninth Symphony or in *Tristan*, will involve not only a great complexity of relationships within
a single key, but a complex of relationships among keys themselves
as extended structural units.

We have so far assumed that various short pieces to which we
have referred remain in one key. But we have also tried to show
that within the limits of one key a considerable variety and range
of harmonies and harmonic relations are possible. Thus, for example, the Bach Prelude (see Appendix, No. 1), the Mozart
Sonatina (see Appendix, No. 4), and the Weber song (see Appendix, No. 5), each of which we will consider as being in one
key throughout, without modulation, involve a greater range or
scope of harmony than either the Leopold Mozart piece or the
Clementi Sonatina (see Appendix, No. 3). This does not, *ipso
facto*, make them greater or better pieces; the point is merely that
they illustrate a variety of possibilities within the limits of relatively simple harmonic organization, and that they all are contained in
a brief span that is nevertheless complete as musical composition.
It is with these pieces that we will begin, since each is clearly and
simply organized, and representative of principles and practices
one encounters over and over again, on smaller and larger scales,
throughout the Classical and Romantic periods. From the particular, as observed in these pieces, one may eventually be able to
generalize.

The very length of a piece, and the speed with which it moves,
are factors in determining the degree of harmonic elaboration possible or desirable within its bounds. A short piece is not usually
found to be elaborate or complex harmonically, but a long piece
almost demands some extension of harmonic and tonal relation-

ships. Beyond simple length and movement, style, as it develops historically, is still more of a factor. It is demonstrable that in the 18th century one is less likely to find harmonic relations extended to remote or subordinate elements or areas of a key, and one never finds them over long periods of time. The 18th-century forms, including the symphony, are notably briefer than those of the 19th century. The structural elements of a key—that is, the connections of unequivocal and easily identifiable tonal sounds such as the tonic and dominant, supertonic and submediant—normally recur with sufficient frequency, and at sufficiently brief intervals, to give the hearer a sense of tonal security and stability. These elements are not as a rule widely separated, as they increasingly tend to be in the 19th century, by chromatic connections, delayed resolutions, or other devices that produce a softening of the structural outlines. It is, of course, just these elaborations that make possible the increased time-span of 19th-century forms. As has already been pointed out, each generation builds on the *hearing* (as well as the acquired technique) of the preceding; and it is assumed in each generation that a further synthetic power is developed for the comprehension of extended harmonic patterns. But even in *Tristan*, which for long passages seems to hover in a tonal limbo, the traditional structural elements are present; they are merely more widely dispersed, and in a sense dissipated, and their connection requires greater attention and memory on the part of the listener.

It may be said again that there are no rules, but only styles. The earlier Classical composers remained closer to their starting keys as a rule, and especially in sonata expositions their key areas and key juxtapositions are most often limited in extent. It is in this aspect of harmonic practice that Beethoven was so original and so powerful. In his expositions, and far more so in his developments, the key exploration as such is on a larger scale than in any music before his, and this is on the whole what accounts for the greater length of Beethoven movements as compared with those of Haydn or Mozart. This, in passing, is exactly what Wagner understood about Beethoven. Whereas other devotees of Beethoven admired the "drama" and other qualities of his music, they did not see as clearly as Wagner how the expressive ends were accomplished.

There are in Beethoven many passages of such rapid and driving harmonic movement that one is hard pressed to follow the relations. The orientation changes as rapidly as one can grasp a point of stability; one is aware of constant activity and kinetic force. Occasionally in Beethoven, and often in Wagner, we feel that we have passages that belong to no key, or to several possible keys, or to any key. The extreme practice of this kind of suspended tonality, as in Wagner, led, as every student now knows, to the eventual rise of the doctrines of pan-tonality or atonality, and to the theoretical formulations of Schoenberg. But until this extreme brings tonality to its own farthest borders, the composer (throughout the 19th century, and certainly through the entire work of Brahms) usually maintains a balance of suspended and stable elements in tonality, and reaffirms, where technically or esthetically necessary, the points of orientation required by the ear trained in the conventional harmonic tradition.

With harmonic and tonal relationships of extreme or relatively great complexity, visual analysis from a score is often helpful in finding logic and connection. But the ear must follow. Often this is difficult, except as the passage of sound in time clarifies what has gone before. This clarification, in visual analysis, may be a deciphering, step by step. Aurally, it cannot be; it is rather a sense of justification, of arrival at the right place; it is felt retrospectively as a satisfaction. In this respect, the key multiplicity, and at times even the uncertainty, of some 19th-century sonata development sections is part of the design. The purpose is to emphasize the order and stability represented by the eventual return to a fixed tonal point.

MODULATION AND SUB-DIVISION

It is true that it is theoretically possible to analyze (visually, if not aurally) any piece of music of the Classical period as being in one key throughout. The attempt will, in most pieces of any size, require some elaborate and casuistical interpretation, and is clearly as a rule no more practical than the results are musically truthful. But they are no more untruthful or unmusical than the opposite extreme of discovering a "modulation" every time an elaboration of an area of the key takes place. Some theorists suggest that whenever a "borrowed" dominant (i.e., a V of V, a V of II, etc.) or dominant seventh occurs, especially at the end of a phrase, the usual resolution of this dominant constitutes in effect a "temporary" or "passing" modulation. On a much broader scale, Roger Sessions employs the term "tonicization" to indicate a temporary point of repose on a note or harmony that is not actually the tonic. These are useful and possible ways of looking at the process, yet they seem to imply a rather more limited sense of key or tonality than is actually experienced in practical hearing. Resting points, on almost any note or step, may simply aid in defining the scope or range of extension and exploration in a simple key scheme, provided always that the ear is able to relate these points to a point of departure and centrality.

KEY "AREA"

The "area" of a key, however, does, even in doctrinaire analysis, have practical limits. If, as we have seen, any chord may occur in a given key and express some relation, however distant, with the tonic, it follows equally that any chord may belong to *any* key. Any triad may be made static, that is, may be made a tonic chord, by means that have been outlined in preceding chapters. But the static triad, or point of aural repose, may be absolute or merely relative. The tonic or static triad in a simple piece is usually clear and unequivocal; one has no doubts about its position or function. But even in simple pieces one usually encounters other resting points, on the dominant or on other more or less closely related triads. To some extent the problem of key and modulation is posed by the degree of repose or finality that the ear (not the eye) attaches to these points of rest.

The capacity for relation will in practice vary from listener to listener, according to training and aural sensibility. It is also true that subtle distinctions are inevitable in matters of this kind, and it should be said at once that there is not always—perhaps even not often—an objective standard or test for determining modulation. Thus, we may have a short piece, a typical A–B–A form, in which the first phrase begins and ends on the tonic, and the second begins and ends on the dominant. Is the second phrase in a new key (that of the dominant) or is it simply a phrase *on* the dominant of the original key? In other words, when, or under what conditions, does such a dominant become a tonic in its own right? This is a question for which, in the abstract, it is almost impossible to provide an answer. Tentatively, one can say that it depends on the ear of the listener almost as much as on the design of the piece. But to balance this, we know that the composers of the 18th and 19th centuries were extremely skillful in the delineation and emphasis of key design of this sort according to their intentions. One is seldom left in doubt when a major change of key, or a return to an original key, is essential to a musical plan.*

HARMONIC PLAN

It is, in any case, the harmonic plan and movement of musical works, especially in the Classical period, to which the listener must in some degree be sensitive. In the tradition of Western music, the composer expects this of the listener, for it is only on this assumption that he can apply his skill or genius to the elaboration of this basic grammar of musical communication. We cannot doubt that the harmonic syntax used and developed over the approximately 250 years from the middle Baroque to the end of the 19th century was felt by all composers of any degree of skill as the primary organizing principle of music and the means by which

* Again Tovey: "Furthermore, I have recently come to realize the enormous amount of collateral evidence that composers with a fine sense of tonality bring to bear upon the listener before they expect him to recognize that a piece of music has returned to its home tonic from a distance." ("Musical Form and Matter," in *The Main Stream of Music*. Meridian Books, 1959.)

measurable segments of time could be organized or shaped into coherent, complete, and meaningful experiences. Without underestimating the roles of melody or rhythm, it must nevertheless be said that both of these are harmonically determined, or, at the very least, that they fit into a fundamentally harmonic way of thinking. Bach's counterpoint is harmonic (and for that reason alone is studied apart from 16th-century counterpoint); it is the harmonic organization that distinguishes it from the equally skillful and ingenious polyphony of Josquin or of Lassus. The fugue differs from the ricercar or the fantasia because it is a harmonically organized work; and the Classical sonata, the characteristic form of its period, is a harmonic form *par excellence*. It is not primarily a melodic form depending on contrast of theme, as is so often and so superficially supposed. (The Classical sonata, in fact, is sometimes almost anti-melodic; it is motivic, sometimes monothematic, usually poly-motivic.) Melody may be memorable or even "inspired" (as it is still customary to say in many instances), yet in fact it cannot and does not during the Classical-Romantic periods escape from a nature and shape given it by dominant-tonic thinking and its extensions. From the smallest piece to the greatest symphony, it is harmonic continuity and logic that is the basis of intelligibility. And harmonic analysis, one must repeat, is useful only insofar as it aids the ear in the understanding of that continuity.

ANALYSIS OF THE CLEMENTI G-MAJOR SONATINA, OPUS 36, NO. 2

Many of these considerations may be illustrated by a very careful examination of even so simple a piece as the G-major Sonatina of Clementi (see Appendix, No. 3), to which the attention of the student is now directed. This familiar little piece has several advantages for our purposes: first, it is representative; and second, it can be played by almost anyone with rudimentary skill at the piano. It can, in fact, be played by two students (non-pianists) on violin and cello, or clarinet and bassoon (with the exception of a very few notes). It is important that it be played, and not merely "analyzed."

The first movement of this Sonatina is analyzed conventionally in the Appendix; that is, the harmonies are identified and named. But it is precisely the inadequacy of such analysis that is the point at issue. The following paragraphs are intended to illustrate some of the points of interest that should be considered:

1. It is evident that we have here a simple piece in G major, and that the harmonic vocabulary is limited to I, VI, II, V, and one easily identified and unambiguous diminished seventh chord. We have, in other words, an almost minimum "area" of harmonic activity for a piece of this length. Taking note of the tempo indication (allegretto), and interpreting this as quarter note 120, we find that the movement takes almost exactly one minute (without repeats) for its 59 measures, or two minutes with the repeats, the importance of which we will discuss directly. Considering absolute speed again, we note that at 120 MM per quarter, each measure takes approximately one second. This is a basic consideration insofar as harmonic design and rate of harmonic change are concerned.

2. The key of G is established in the first four measures, as follows:

$$I \mid I \mid V \mid I$$

This is one of the simplest and most usual four-measure formulas in traditional practice. Note that the theme, or more properly "motif," is triadic.

The following four measures give us: I | VI | II (V of V) | V, and constitute a motivic repetition of the first four, with the phrase ending on the dominant. We have no thought at this point that we are anywhere but in the key of G. Our *anticipation* at this point is open to a continuation on I or on any nearly related triad. What happens in fact is that we hear next four measures of V, followed by a cadence of VI–II (V of V) – V (measures 13–14); these six measures are followed by six almost identical measures (four measures of V, two measures of II–V cadence); the exposition section then ends on a strongly established dominant (D).

The question here is one of great importance in the study of traditional harmonic design, and applies to works of far greater dimension than this Sonatina movement. It is this: is there a point at which we feel that the V becomes a tonic, and, if so, *when* does this occur? In other words, does this small exposition section *modulate* from G to D and if so, at what point, or do we hear it simply as closing on the dominant of G?

It would appear that, on the very limited scale of the work, a modulation to the dominant is indeed intended. But (and especially on this small scale) the relation I to V (G to D) is so close that it is difficult to say where one establishes a relative independence of the other, or where the *key* of one ends and the other begins. Does the ear accept the V throughout as a part of the larger unity of I, or does it re-orient itself to D as a new tonic? The evidence for a new key center includes the comparative length (14 measures as opposed to 8) of dwelling on D, the emphatic use of the V of D, and particularly the repetition (in measures 20–21) of a strong dominant-tonic conclusion. But even this need not be conclusive.

It may be conceded that an argument or protracted discussion of this point is in large part academic. We hear the piece, and find it coherent, and it may seem sheer pedantry to attempt a verbal decision on a moot point. Nevertheless, by using this ambiguity as a point of departure, we are able to consider some related problems of traditional harmonic structure, especially as they concern the sonata form.

3. Some light on traditional practice is immediately afforded by considering a matter usually neglected both in "analysis" and in performance: the fact that the exposition of almost every Classical sonata or sonatina is designed to be repeated. (This holds true, incidentally, of the majority of sonata-form works up to and in-

cluding Brahms; it is not merely an 18th-century mannerism.) Several conclusions may be drawn from this. First, that the ending of the exposition, whether it is in the tonic, the dominant, or some other key, must lead back to the opening (tonic) as well as onward to the development. It will therefore usually be not far removed tonally from the tonic. If a modulation to the dominant has in effect taken place, the relation back to the tonic is perfectly simple and clear. In early Classical sonatas the ending of the exposition was generally designed to work both ways, to the beginning of the movement (in other words, to the *second* exposition), or to the development. But it will be noted that as the exposition becomes more involved tonally, first and second endings are found to be necessary. What seems to be the case here is that if by length or tonal extension the movement has got rather far away from the tonic, a brief connection is needed to lead back to the opening. Occasionally, it would even appear necessary to "modulate" back to the tonic.* The student should examine a number of expositions in works of Haydn, Mozart, Beethoven, and others, noting well the connection of the end of the exposition with its opening as well as its following development. The harmonic linkage is important, but even more important is the fact that composers, through repetition, evidently wished their hearers to have a firmly established sense of the point of tonal departure (the tonic) partly in order that they might more fully appreciate the harmonic variety and extension of a development.

4. Even on the small scale of the Clementi Sonatina we see that the actuality of modulation hinges on factors of time and of emphasis. *Modulation is not schematic*, and the schematizing of

---

* In this connection, see the article "A Musical Mutilation" by Leonard Marcus in *Juilliard Review*, Vol. IV, No. 3, Fall 1957. Mr. Marcus conclusively demonstrates the importance of the repeat of the exposition from the harmonic and structural viewpoints, and underlines the fact that contemporary audiences (for various reasons) are seldom given the opportunity of hearing first endings as the composers obviously intended they should.

modulatory formulas is misleading. The introduction of any new dominant seventh chord can suggest the possibility of movement to another key, but on the other hand it may, in a musical rather than a schematic context, be found to function solely to emphasize a certain triad in the given key. One cannot construct modulating formulas that will automatically "work"; their efficiency depends on musical context. *Modulation is a carefully planned relation in time*, depending on (1) the establishment of a point of departure, (2) a process of motion towards another point, and (3) the confirmation of the new point or tonal center. This last, in Classical and Romantic sonata form, is usually, though not invariably, marked by a new "theme" or subject.

As an example of forceful and unmistakable modulation in an exposition section, we may examine the C-major (*Waldstein*) Sonata of Beethoven, a work of large scale and a most striking example of immense harmonic power magnificently controlled and directed. The schematic outline of harmonic succession is extremely simple, and may be reduced to the following:

Ex. 82

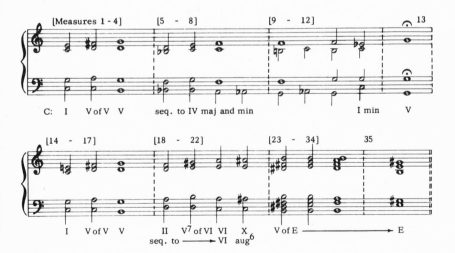

This outline of course does not tell the story. In terms of chord progression, the movement to E major is accomplished by exactly two chords: one augmented sixth and a dominant seventh on B. But these are only the basic tools of the modulation. In order to make the change to E effective, so that no one hearing the Sonata can be in any doubt whatsoever, Beethoven insists on the V^7 of E for no fewer than twelve full measures of unswerving emphasis. One may describe this as a crescendo of expectation. When the V^7 resolves on E major, and the second subject is presented, a grand harmonic design has been accomplished. The mechanism of chord connection could hardly be simpler, but the calculation of force and time is the proof of artistic mastery. The first and second endings of the exposition section should also be studied as examples of harmonic planning and direction.*

5. Returning to the Clementi, it will be noted that the second part of the movement, comprising the development and the recapitulation, is also repeated. We have here the same interesting problem of design: the recommencement of a section from a different point of departure. But it is to be noted that the development begins as if it were to be identical with the opening, with the principal motif in the tonic. It is thus equally approachable from tonic or dominant.† But the harmony shifts, on the last eighth note of the measure with the introduction of the G♯ and the F, outlining a diminished seventh chord, G♯–B–D–F (the ear carrying over the B and the D), which resolves in the most direct manner to a triad on A, or II of the key of G. In measure 29, a "half-diminished" seventh F♯–A–C–E (with E proceeding to D) leads

---

* To emphasize that the technique of modulation is never simple, and that there are many varieties of effective practice in the masters, one may examine the Piano Sonata K. 284 or the String Quartet K. 575 of Mozart, both in D, in which the first sections of the expositions seem to "modulate" to A. In each work the recapitulation repeats this first section, *but remains in D.*

† This is the essential point; if at the end of the exposition or beginning of the development one had really modulated away from the center, would one not have to modulate back? One would in such a case need first and second endings.

to a resolution on G, after which we have a re-establishment and confirmation of G, via VI, II, and V. In the development we have, in other words, a going *backward* to II, so as to gain a slightly greater distance from which to return to G, or I.

This technique is used again and again in the Classical sonata. Developments repeatedly take off from points more or less distant from the tonic, and proceed back to the tonic by directly related stages.

In the case of the Clementi, as with many larger Classical and Romantic works, the effectiveness of the *change* at the beginning of the development is greatly enhanced by the repetition of the exposition. It is unfortunate indeed that in most performances today the repetition of the exposition is omitted, thus depriving audiences (as well as performers) of one of the principal pivots of interest in sonata design.

6. One further point may be made about the harmonic treatment of development sections. (It is not apparent in the Clementi, but is often found in larger works.) Where harmonic movement is directed, as suggested above, from a relatively distant point back to a tonic, movement may be extremely rapid, and may touch on intermediate points very fleetingly. Indeed, in many instances (for example, the Beethoven F-major String Quartet, Opus 18, No. 1), a passage back from III to I (A major to F major) may touch on VI and II only by suggestion, through the use of diminished seventh chords (as VII⁷) or similar devices.* But in all instances the point of termination, that is, the original tonic, will be made explicit and emphatic. Thus, in the Beethoven Quartet just mentioned, the return to F and its stabilization are made clear through twelve measures of strongly affirmed dominant seventh on C. The ear cannot go astray with this guidance.

---

* See the Brahms *Intermezzo*, Opus 76, No. 4, in B♭ (see Appendix No. 13) for an example of the establishment of tonality almost exclusively through the use of the V⁷, with no reference to I until the very end.

7. There are other conventions to be remarked in the Clementi example, and these too may be extended and applied to larger works. The student will note the use of scale passages at many points. Here he will have to decide, as suggested in Chapter I, which notes are passing tones. The harmonic outline in this instance is so clear that he will have no trouble. But scales are often used in traditional practice simply to outline a harmony, and the question of passing tones becomes rather subordinate. Again, in the Beethoven F-major Quartet, scales are used effectively at many points, notably the C-major scales at the end of the exposition, to emphasize the stability of the key.

In the Clementi most of the scale passages contain accented harmonic tones and unaccented passing tones. The important exceptions are in measures 19 and 55, where the accented fourths are non-harmonic, and the harmonies are understood as formed by the following thirds.

The student should also take note of the way in which a harmonic change is effected in measure 31. The beginning of the measure sounds unquestionably as an E-minor triad (VI of G, a "deceptive" cadence following the implied V⁷ of the previous measure), but the C♯ on the last sixteenth note of the measure transforms the harmony in a rapid but direct stroke to an implied V of V, returning to V. This type of application of a transforming leading-tone is common in traditional practice, and the student should look for similar examples.* Equally common is the transformation of a dominant seventh to a diminished seventh by moving the root a half step upward.

8. The final point to be noted in the Clementi is the absolute importance of the two eighths of *rest* in measure 36. Perhaps this is the most important lesson in harmony to be derived from the study of this Sonatina. For quite clearly, nothing matters here but a passage of *time*, perhaps half a second for the ear to make its

* An almost identical example will be found in the Bach chorale *Liebster Jesu* (see Appendix, No. 10), measure 6, 3rd quarter.

adjustment to the V⁷ of G implied by the two voices on D and C (the F♯ and A have been heard in the previous measure), and to balance expectantly for the final reaffirmation of G. The use of the rest is the most difficult musical manipulation to teach students of composition; yet meaningful silence is surely one of the most notable characteristics of design in music. Here in this Clementi piece we have a very simple indication of how important and effective the rest may be in harmonic structure.*

The rest may also serve to mark what may be described as an "elision" in harmonic continuity. Note the following, from the second movement of the D-minor Quartet, K. 421, of Mozart:

Ex. 83

* Note also the function of the one-measure rest in the Schubert *Moment musical* (see Appendix, No. 7).

These are surely among the most beautiful rests in all of musical literature (and I should add that they must be beautifully *performed!*). It is to be hoped that the student will understand without difficulty how crucially important here is the question of tempo: how a carefully considered and measured pace alone enables the ear to follow the intricacies of the flow from the harmony of D major (VI) back to F (I), through the pivotal bar with the rests. In a good performance, the ear accepts the F as final, as unquestionably I. In a sense, the II that might have come between the VI and the V to make the complete cadence, is *elided* and represented by the first two eighth rests. But whether or not this interpretation is acceptable, the fact remains that the rests are (figuratively speaking) the most important sounds in the phrase. It may be said that a large part of the *art* of music is represented by what is seen and heard here in microcosm. For this is a very high achievement in giving meaning to time, and in imposing control over time to achieve expressiveness.

10. It remains to sum up the total harmonic structure of the Sonatina. The analysis by chord identification in the Appendix provides a detail of progression from measure to measure, but this detail, essential as it is, may in fact obscure more important harmonic divisions. We have already suggested, in connection with the Leopold Mozart Polonaise (see Chapter II and Appendix) that the division I–V–I within its first and second measures is in effect a subdivision, and that the measures may properly be construed as I. We tend to hear harmonic divisions on varying scales, depending again on speed and proportion. As hearing becomes more developed and sophisticated, larger outlines take on clarity, while we become at the same time more sensitive to the subdivisions that give movement and variety within their spans. Thus the first four measures of the Sonatina (I–I–V–I) may be taken as a simple statement (extension or elaboration) of I, and the Sonatina as a whole may be construed at its simplest as follows:

Section A: ||: I (4 measures) | I to V (4 measures) | V (14 measures) :||
Section B: ||: II (6 measures) | V (8 measures) |
Section C: I (23 measures) :||

This is what is essential in the harmonic plan.

A procedure of attempting to find the simplest over-all harmonic pattern in this manner is helpful not only in perceiving the shape or form of an entire piece, but also, in most cases, in placing and understanding the detail. It is on the whole a much more reward-ing and musical procedure to begin with the larger aspects of a harmonic structure, thence proceeding to an analysis of detail, than it is to begin with the detail itself. It is in the minutiae of de-tail that analysis often gets lost and defeats itself.

The time and space given to the study of one movement of a Clementi Sonatina are justified, one hopes, by the inferences to be drawn from it, and perhaps also because the study indicates a method of analysis and study by comparison and extension. The Clementi itself may be appreciated as a well-designed miniature, the logic and balance of which are easy to perceive, and which is written unpretentiously with a complete ease in a language natural to its composer. This language, even at its simplest, as here, is not without its subtleties and refinements. The student should now undertake a similar careful study of the second movement of the Sonatina, which he will also find in the Appendix (No. 3). He should play it before beginning to "analyze" it, paying attention to the dynamics and other marks of expression, and considering care-fully the question of tempo. He may then begin by defining the harmonic structure in general and in detail, noting the construc-tion of the first four-measure phrase and the subdivisions within the measures, as he hears them.

A next step may well be the consideration of the first movement of the "Viennese Sonatina" in A of Mozart.* This is no longer

* Mozart's "Viennese" Sonatinas were adapted from Serenades (or Divertimenti) originally written for basset-horns and bassoon, K. 439. They were transcribed by an unknown hand for piano after Mozart's death, and published in this form by Artaria. They are genuine enough for our purposes.

than the Clementi movement, but it is obviously larger in harmonic scope. Again to be considered is the question of modulation in the exposition, which clearly progresses from I to V, and the return to the opening or the continuation to the development. The opening of the development section is interesting for the sequence involved. We go immediately from the sound of E major at the end of the exposition to the sound of C major. The effect is fresh and momentarily disorienting: the relation to either E or A is, *on the scale of the piece,* rather distant. But the re-orientation is delightful. We can know only in retrospect (we are speaking always of the ear, not the eye) that C major is N⁶ of II, that the progression is N⁶ of II, V of II, *II* (of which we have two measures, for balance and stability); then N⁶ (of I), V, and I. We have, in other words, an artful and sophisticated elaboration of II–V–I. But we are not aware of this until the entire sequence has unfolded.

Let us examine the same type of sequence, considerably extended, in Beethoven:

Ex. 84   Beethoven: Piano Sonata, Op. 10, No. 2

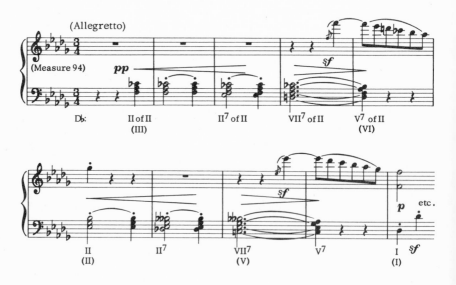

This sequence involves overlapping, extension, and a type of chromatic movement that is characteristic of 19th-century practice. It may be "diagrammed" as follows:

Ex. 85

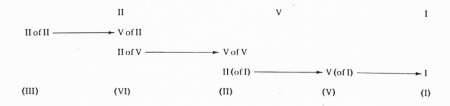

To be noted here, aside from the pattern of the sequence, is the alteration of chords by half steps:

F–Ab–Cb–Eb

F–Ab–Cb–D

F–Ab–Bb–D   etc.

Another favorite device of Beethoven, much used by Schumann also, is the rapid change of dominant sevenths through half-step motion in one or another voice, as in the following:

Ex. 86   Schumann: *Valse noble* (meas. 24–28)

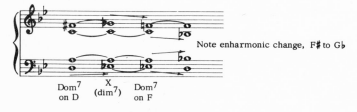

Beethoven: Piano Sonata, Op. 90

(meas. 29–45)   (meas. 50–55)

The *Lied* by Carl Maria von Weber (see Appendix, No. 5) is on a different scale, and should also be studied carefully at this point. Weber is neglected today, and his importance in the development of style in the early 19th century is generally ignored. We have in this 16-measure song a remarkable example of the "dimension" of Weber's harmony, and of what was, in its time, a highly personal and novel use of dominant seventh chords. As noted in Chapter V, the phrase structure of the piece is also of considerable interest, and the balanced and effective use of the IV (as "antidominant") is noteworthy. The harmonic "area" of the work extends as far as V^7 of III, remarkable in so short a piece, but admirably effective. The dominant ninth in measure 10 is relatively pure, but falls back, as is so often the case, into the dominant seventh. In measure 13, the voice (2nd eighth) makes a dominant ninth with the piano part, but this is clearly a passing sound. This type of sound, exceptionally liquid and sonorous, is one of the marks of Weber's style.

A more interesting problem in analysis is the Mozart Adagio, from the *Adagio and Allegro for a Musical Clockwork*, K. 594 (see Appendix, No. 6). Much of this will be discussed in the next chapter. It is mentioned at this point because the student can see in it an example of a still more greatly enlarged area of a key. The Adagio is in F, and does not modulate to C, although it closes on the C-major triad. (It is impossible for anyone with a sensitive ear to begin a movement in C after the fermata; it is clearly a dominant of F, and demands a continuation in F.) The Adagio is short, 39 measures, and taking the Adagio at 56 MM per quarter note, extends for approximately two minutes. It is full of interest harmonically, a fine example of Mozart's mature art, and is an excellent introduction to the study of developed chromatic harmony.

Assignments:

The student may study and analyze Nos. 7, 8, 9, 10, and 11 in the Appendix, from the standpoints of harmonic detail and of over-all structure and form. He should in addition examine and analyze works such as the following (he should, of course, *hear* these works first!):

1. Sonatinas of Clementi, Mozart, Beethoven, and others of the period.
2. Sonata in C major (B.&H. No. 33) of Haydn.
3. Sonata in F major (K. 332) of Mozart.
4. Sonata in F major, Opus 10, No. 2, of Beethoven.
5. Sonata in C major, Opus 24, of Weber.
6. If able to read quartet score, String Quartet, Opus 18, No. 1, of Beethoven.

Exercises:

After sufficient study of a selection of the works listed above, the student should attempt to compose:

1. A sonatina movement in the style of Clementi.
2. A song (with or without words) in the style of the Weber example.

Chapter Ten

*Chromaticism—Stylistic Development from
Monteverdi to Wagner*

CHROMATICISM—STYLISTIC DEVELOPMENT
FROM MONTEVERDI TO WAGNER

Chromaticism is inherent in traditional Western harmony from
the moment the raised third in the V of V becomes a part of the
basic vocabulary of tonally organized music. Its use in such a manner is found in Monteverdi, as for example in his Seventh Book of
Madrigals (1619):

Ex. 87   Monteverdi: Sinfonia to *Tempro la Cetra*

The development of this principle and the introduction of the
diminished seventh as a common chord of unrestricted use involve
the use of all twelve tones even in many simple pieces limited to
relatively small areas of a single key. It is, however, true that the
twelve notes may be used in a piece that will not ordinarily be described as "chromatic," as, for example, the Bach C-major Prelude.
What we describe as "chromatic" harmony results from other

procedures that have to do with extension in time as well as in harmonic vocabulary.

Chromaticism is often understood to be that type of melodic and harmonic movement characterized by an abundance (or even a preponderance) of movement by semitones or half steps. This type of movement is indeed characteristic of Wagnerian or Franckian harmony, yet much more is involved. The idea of a flux, of a constant shifting, through the use of half steps, is a matter of esthetic as well as of technique, and the exploitation of the tendencies of raised tones to continue upward (and of lowered tones to continue downward) becomes part of an expressive manner that seeks to extend motion, and the boundaries of musical measure, towards the infinite.

The technical handling of chromatic elements is always subordinate to an esthetic limitation: it is not merely a matter of chords, or of raised and lowered melodic tones. Bach used most of the chords in Wagner's vocabulary; Mozart, Haydn, and Beethoven all knew the expressive power of the chromaticized passage. But the ideal of classical art has always been containment or boundary, and all of the Classical masters including Beethoven respected a self-imposed tonal limitation. (Beethoven, it is true, stretched the limits considerably.) The following passage from the *Orgelbüchlein* of Bach is illuminating:

Ex. 88   Bach: Chorale Prelude,
   O Mensch, bewein' dein' Sünde gross

This remarkable passage does not depart from its key of E♭, yet it embraces an enormous range of harmonic movement, and is fully "chromatic" for much of its length. One sees and hears clearly the pivotal points of structure; there is an evident distinction between structural and non-structural cadences. The principal divisions of the section quoted come to full cadences on VI (V of II), II (V of V), V, and I. This is the very model of classical construction, strictly delimited, yet these pivotal points are connected by extraordinarily rich and varied movement—movement, moreover, that illustrates many of the basic processes of chromatic harmony with perfect clarity. One hears seventh chords resolving to seventh chords, or dominant sevenths changing to diminished sevenths, as illustrated in preceding chapters. One hears, also, successions of "deceptive" resolutions, and stepwise sequences constructed with interpolated dominants (as described in Chapter VII). These are all characteristic movements of chromatic harmony, to be found again and again in Beethoven, Schumann, Chopin, Wagner, and almost all middle and late 19th-century composers.

The passage beginning with measure 3 is particularly to be noted. A harmony of V^7 of IV (E♭–G–D♭) becomes, by half-step motion, a V^7 of II (E♮–G–B♭–C), and resolves expectedly to a harmony on the root F, in this case a dominant seventh. This in turn, by half-step motion (F–A–C–E♭ to F♯–A–C–D), becomes a dominant seventh on D. When the D returns to E♭, the harmony becomes a diminished seventh (VII^7 of G). Whether one hears these as separate harmonies, or as aspects of one harmony, or as a single harmony with a passing tone, will depend on many variable factors, including performance, or on subjective elements of hearing. All analytical possibilities may be justified; the logic of connection remains evident throughout, from the smallest element in the chain to the largest unit of phrase construction.

The last few measures of the Prelude are perhaps even more striking. Here one finds a series of dominant sevenths on E♭ (V^7 of IV), F (V^7 of V), and G (V^7 of VI), each of which proceeds to a "deceptive" resolution stepwise, to F, G, and A♭ respectively (II, III, and IV), making an upward stepwise sequence of precisely the type used so often by Wagner. At the end of measure 7, there is a triad on the lowered sixth (C♭), which may be described as V of N, followed by N^6 (with a minor II interposed), then a diminished seventh on D♮ (VII⁷) converted by the change of D to E♭ into a minor II⁷,* and thence proceeding with marvelous effect to a strong cadence of I$^6_4$, V⁷, I.†

Harmonic changes of this complexity and subtlety must have time in which to evolve and to be perceived, and the tempo of this Chorale Prelude, even without the indications of *Adagio assai* and *Adagissimo*, can be clearly felt as one of the greatest deliberation.‡ One must feel *simultaneously* every harmonic division and sub-division, from the broad phrase structure of I–VI–II–V–I of the passage as a whole, down to the minute shading of change by six-teenth note. There are in one sense not many notes in this passage that can be characterized with certainty as passing tones, and yet, in another sense, all except the pivotal harmonies are passing. This is the paradox and the subtlety of such music as this.

Equally subtle and yet equally clear is the Mozart Adagio (see Appendix, No. 6) to which reference has already been made. Here too is an example of chromatic harmony that is controlled, or "bounded," by traditional principles of time organization and tonal structure, and that nevertheless points the way towards the mid-19th century's development of chromaticism as the organizing principle of new musical forms.

The Adagio is unmistakably in F (minor), and it does not modulate, although it closes on a strongly established dominant (which is preparation for the following Allegro section in F major). The Adagio itself is another of those many works that fluctuate between major and minor, or include both. To be noted at the

---

* This alteration of diminished seventh on the leading-tone to minor II⁷, and vice versa, is found frequently from Bach through Brahms. It has seldom been given much theoretical notice, yet it suggests an extension of the idea that the diminished seventh on the leading tone is an incomplete dominant ninth. The V⁷, VII⁷, and II⁷ all overlap, or, to take the notion to its extreme, are all found in the dominant eleventh. The minor II (a diminished triad) seems occasionally to assume a dominant function, as if it were a substitute for, or were to be understood as, an incomplete VII⁷. It seems to operate in this manner in the Brahms Intermezzo in B♭ minor (see discussion in Appendix, No. 14).

† The context and effect of the major triad on C♭ here should be compared with those of the C♭ major triad in Act II of *Tristan* (p. 162, Breitkopf vocal score). The similarities are striking, as are, of course, the differences.

‡ Problem: to set a metronomic speed for the eighth-note unit.

outset is the chromatically descending bass of the first six measures, repeated, in diminution, in upper voices (measures 29 and 31) and in the bass again (measure 33). The first six measures include a diminished seventh and an augmented sixth chord, a major IV, and at the close of the phrase a cadence on V overlapped by its own VII⁷, treated as an appoggiatura. But there are again questions of tempo and of subjective hearing as well as of conventional harmonic analysis. The fifth measure will illustrate this. We have the clear impression of the single measure as the harmonic unit in measures 1, 2, and 3. In measure 4, the possibility of a change on the third quarter is suggested. Does the major IV change to a VII, or do we hear and construe the G in the top voice as a passing tone and the E♮ in the third voice as a simple neighboring tone? It is again probably not possible to say with certainty. The connection to the first quarter of the following measure is equally logical with either construction. These analytical constructions are in any case important only insofar as they explain the reasons why the movement is smooth and convincing to the ear. The fifth measure poses the same problem somewhat more elaborately. The first vertical configuration of the measure has the sound of an augmented sixth chord ("German"), and a look at the movement of the bass seems to confirm this impression. The D♭ and the B♮ move to the dominant octave of C, as can be clearly heard. Yet there is a possibility that on the third quarter we do not actually hear an augmented sixth: the B♮ and G suggest V of V, and the continued motion on the last eighth note suggests a change to a diminished seventh on B♮. (This is, in fact, the sound that is carried over to the following measure.) What is interesting here is again the impossibility of a rigid and doctrinaire "analysis" without taking into account factors of tempo and—most pointedly, even on an instrument as non-accentual as the organ—the feeling and understanding of the performer. In a unitary harmonic sense, the three possible chords heard in the measure are all forms of the dominant of the dominant; we are again faced with the constantly interesting problem of division and subdivision. But the augmented sixth, the V of V, and the VII^7 of V all clearly feed our expectation of the V, in different degrees, and this kind of change is one of the principal mechanisms of chromaticism. Here this mechanism is shown simply and clearly; how beautiful, logical, and subtle it is!

In measures 8–11 we have a first inversion series with suspensions, leading to a somewhat inconclusive cadence on I. (One feels the V as rather stronger than the I; the inconclusiveness or ambiguity here is also typical of later stylistic developments: Wagner characteristically leads the hearer to a cadence and then refuses to confirm it.) Structurally this is most important, for the Adagio then expands through a diffused motion toward A♭ (measures 12–20), B♭ (measures 20–24), and C, the dominant (measures 24–28), the last two in sequence.

The section from measure 12 through measure 20 is full of interest, again from the standpoint of division and subdivision, and also from the standpoint of suggested (and deployed) harmony, and the placing of non-harmonic tones. Measure 15 is a case in point. The E♭ is a non-harmonic chromatic passing tone (but strongly accented); the F♭ and D♮ suggest a dominant seventh on B♭, with diminished fifth, changing in the next measure to a suggestion of the same chord with natural fifth, in both cases a V^7 of V, or II^7 with relation to A♭. But it is not until measure 19 that this dominant seventh (for that is what it in effect proves to be) resolves unambiguously and finally to the V^7 (on E♭). The resolution is delayed, again a mannerism of later style, by the interposition of three diminished seventh chords, and by suspensions in the upper voice. The chromatic downward movement of the third voice should also be particularly noted.

Diminished seventh chords are also a feature of the progressions in measures 33–35. In measure 33, one should note the compression (or diminution) of the entire harmonic progression originally heard in measures 1–6. Here each original measure is represented by an eighth note: six eighth notes for six measures. In measures 34 and 35, the pedal-point on the dominant (C) is also to be noted. As usual with pedal-points, this C should not be accounted a structural part of the harmonies evolving above it; but like all pedal-points, it is not without effect on the harmonic sound and over-all phrase structure. Of the diminished seventh chords heard above it, all except the first one on A♮, resolving to IV, are VII⁷'s of V, functioning as dominants of the dominant. It may be observed here how much less force these have as final cadence progressions than seventh chords on the dominant itself, true V's or V⁷'s.

In measures 29 and 31, Mozart transforms a minor II into an N⁶ in almost exactly the same way we have noted in the Bach example above. For the remaining points in connection with the Mozart, the reader is referred to the notes and analysis in the Appendix.

Several conclusions may be drawn from the examination of these examples from Bach and Mozart. It can be seen that one primary mechanism of chromaticism is the transformation of a chord to a chord similar in function by movement of a half step in one or sometimes two voices. We have seen, as examples, movement from minor II to N⁶, augmented sixth to V of V, V⁷ to VII⁷ and vice versa. The Mozart also illustrates the chromatic possibilities of major-minor alternation. Both the Bach and the Mozart show the chromatic possibilities inherent in the uses of N⁶ and of V of N or other applications and dominant extensions of triads on lowered second or sixth degrees. In the Mozart, we have also seen the effect, in changing harmonies, of suspensions and of appoggiatura chords, as well as of the pedal-point.

The relation of these passages to later stylistic developments is evident, and it is not an exaggeration to state that the road from these examples to the techniques and style of *Tristan* or *Parsifal* is clearly indicated. What makes this clear is not only the verifiable likeness of the harmonies employed, but their manner of linear connection, and their deployment in a contrapuntal fabric involving continual harmonic change. The suspensions and other non-harmonic tones in the Mozart are typical of a mannerism in late chromatic style; the procedure is carried to its extreme in Wagner, whose progressions are elaborated by non-harmonic tones, often very long-held and not resolved until their harmonic points of gravitation have themselves been changed. However, whereas in Bach or Mozart there are many simple triads, especially VI, II, V, and I, serving as points of tonal orientation, these become fewer and farther apart in much of Wagner, and indeed are at times so far apart that one loses all sense of tonal firmness or security. The Wagnerian lines tend to form configurations with few static chords; the harmonies are in large part moving and dynamic—sevenths, augmented sixths, or simpler chords with sharply dissonant non-harmonic tones—with no end of the motion in sight. With this kind of motion and sound, continually restless, it is often impossible to identify chords as such; many of them represent passing and rapidly changing configurations between points that are in themselves passing and changing.

The identification of chords as such by nomenclature is not a matter of great importance. Far too much stress is generally placed upon this purely academic exercise. Even in so simple an example as the following,

Ex. 89   Robert Franz: *Wie des Mondes Abbild*

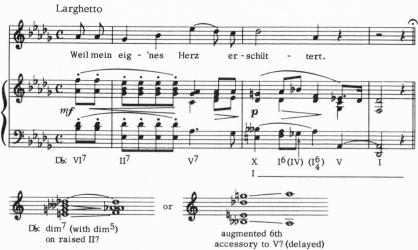

we run into difficulties of nomenclature or descriptive terminology. An excellent musician and theorist describes the chord at X as "a diminished seventh with doubly diminished fifth," which is no doubt etymologically plausible, but tells us little. The description indicates that it is an "altered" diminished seventh chord on the raised supertonic,* but gives no hint of reason or function. Nor, for that matter, does another possibility, that it is a chord of the doubly augmented fourth (B♭♭–D♭–E–G), help us much, except that we can verify that the augmented sixth interval does in fact resolve to the dominant octave, A♭–A♭. What the chord is called makes no difference whatever; its function is clear and its effect is striking. It extends and elaborates, by chromatic movement, a simple V⁷–I progression. It is neither a passing chord nor an appoggiatura chord; it is essentially a chord of connection, extension, or elaboration, but is not a chord of primary structural importance.

Chords such as this are generally best understood as groups of neighboring or passing notes (sometimes appoggiaturas) that are interpolated as extensions and connections between harmonies of greater (though not necessarily primary) significance. It is neither necessary nor helpful to attempt to find names for them, unless the name itself—as, for example, dominant seventh—is immediately suggestive of a primary function.

Chords that are employed as extensions or interpolations are, in the 18th and early 19th centuries, generally resolved, or led to a resolution, within a short time-span. In all cases, they are directed towards a point that is not distant, and to which a relation is seldom hard to perceive. With the development of later 19th-century style, these chords are often extended in time, or several of them may occur in succession, with the result that basic tonal

---

* Some theorists make a special case of the diminished seventh on the raised supertonic and submediant, adding them to the already cluttered store of formally classified "altered" chords. Since the chords usually behave like any other diminished sevenths, dependent upon context, there seems to be no reason for giving them special attention. As has been noted, diminished seventh chords can, and do, occur on any of the twelve tones, in any key.

processes are temporarily in abeyance. The "connecting" harmonies become themselves the objects of attention and protraction. The result is often a suspension of any sense of tonality or tonal direction. Uncertainty or ambiguity of this sort is exploited effectively all through the 19th century. (It is almost never found in Bach or Haydn, but is occasionally suggested in Mozart.) The diminished seventh, being rootless except where its structure is made explicit by context, is of course one of the harmonies most frequently exploited in ambiguous passages of this sort. The Chopin Mazurka (see Appendix, No. 16) illustrates a real suspension of tonality in measures 13–15 of the section given; the three successive diminished sevenths give little clue to their eventual destination. It may indeed be suggested that one is not in any identifiable key from measure 7 onward; not until measures 16–18, when we have unmistakable N^6–V–I, is a sense of key firmly established.

This example from Chopin is, as has been suggested in Chapter VIII, very close in technique to Wagner, the chief difference being one of scale. The indeterminate harmony in Chopin is never maintained for more than a few measures, and Chopin's essentially traditional manner of thinking always persuades him to confirm a key center within a relatively brief time. But the passage given is full of "Wagnerian" mannerisms: the diminished sevenths, the ambiguous augmented sixths (spelled with a concern for visual convenience rather than structural accuracy), and the elaborately ornamented sequences that do not reveal themselves readily, are all characteristic of Wagner's style, as are the Neapolitan harmonies (often in root position) and the ninths, so often falling, after a delay, into sevenths. Also characteristic, in measure 9, is the "half-diminished" seventh F–A♭–C♭–E♭ (minor II^7 of E♭) moving through an augmented sixth chord (C♭–A♮) to a second inversion of the E♭ triad, itself not a static sound. (See further analysis in Appendix.)

These movements bring up the question of what many theorists term "irregular" resolutions. It is incontestably true in many passages of Chopin and Wagner (as well as of many other earlier and later composers) that seventh chords and even augmented sixth chords do not seem to proceed in "expected" directions. But the "expectation" is, as we have tried to show, a matter of convention rather than of acoustics, or of style rather than technique. These "irregular" resolutions are "regular" in Wagner; or to put it in reverse, what is "regular" in Wagner, Chopin, or Liszt would perhaps be highly irregular in Bach or Handel.* Again Tovey puts the matter well when he states that "the pleasure given by every effort at revolutionary harmony results from the fact that the new chords enter our consciousness with the meaning they would bear in a classical scheme. . . . Bach and Palestrina lurk behind every new harmonic sensation." † Tovey might well have added that it is not only "new chords" (of which, in reality, there are not many), but even more the new contexts and applications found for the same chordal sounds.

For the heart of the matter is not "irregular" resolution or new chords, but the acceptance and exploitation of ambiguities inherent in exactly similar sounds with varying functions. It has been suggested in Chapter VIII that all of the seventh chords, for example, may be used equivocally or unequivocally. Classical usage is generally of the latter style; "romantic" (or middle and late 19th-century) usage is very often of the former. A diminished or "half-diminished" seventh chord in Bach is most often directly resolved, functioning as a VII to a following harmony. But in Wagner, the "half-diminished" seventh chord, one of his most heavily exploited harmonic sounds, may be a II or a VII or merely a connection to

---

* Bach's Chorale Preludes, especially those of the early period in Arnstadt, contain many "irregular" resolutions and progressions, as well as startling chromaticisms, that are well worth study. From the standpoint of expressive intent, in which respect a comparison with Wagner is not unthinkable, these works are of particular interest.

† Tovey, *The Forms of Music.*

a more explicit harmony. It may, as in the following, from *Parsifal,* be an accessory to a dominant seventh:

Ex. 90 Wagner: *Parsifal,* Act II
(Kleinmichel piano reduction, p. 196)

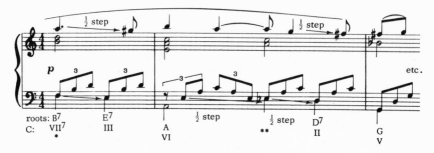

*"half-diminished" 7th on B, embellishing dominant 7th on E.
**"half-diminished" 7th on A, embellishing dominant 7th on D.

We may compare the "half-diminished" F–Ab–Cb–Eb noted above in the Chopin Mazurka with the same four notes in *Parsifal:*

Ex. 91 Wagner: *Parsifal,* Act II (Eulenburg orchestral score, p. 264)

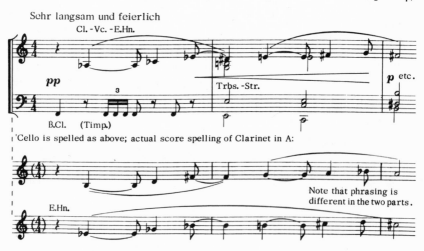

'Cello is spelled as above; actual score spelling of Clarinet in A:

Note that phrasing is different in the two parts.

The chords in Chopin and Wagner contain the identical notes, and both "read" as "half-diminished" sevenths. But they are nevertheless not the same, either in the sound that the differing contexts give them, or in their resolutions.

The full passage from *Parsifal* is given in the Appendix, No. 19, and the student will note that on its recurrence the chord F–A♭–C♭–E♭ is spelled F–G♯–B–D♯. The sound is exactly the same, but in the second instance, the chord appears to be a "new" type of augmented sixth, and with the resolution to an E minor triad (the F and the D♯ proceeding outward to E–E) this interpretation seems justified. But the resolution is also the same in the first instance! The spelling is further complicated by the transpositions necessary in the orchestral score. The clarinet in A, for example, reads the A♭–C♭–E♭ as B–D–F♯, and the player probably thinks of the concert pitch as G♯–B–D♯. We thus see that there is a certain arbitrariness about spelling, but it is based in every case on equal temperament. There can be no real distinction between G♯ and A♭ in this kind of musical thinking. Nor can there, for this reason, be a real question of cataloguing or categorizing many of the harmonic configurations that occur. The chord in question from *Parsifal*, from the way it moves, should most accurately be spelled F–A♭–B–D♯ (or, reading in thirds: B–D♯–F–A♭), which would indeed be a new chord. The temptation to find a label for it is one to be resisted. We are justified in explaining it and understanding it only in terms of its dynamic properties—that is, the tendencies of its components to move onward in aurally comprehensible steps.

If the sound of the "half-diminished" seventh chord may become as equivocal as we have just seen, we should not be surprised to find that even the ordinary dominant seventh is often transformed in Wagnerian contexts. The end of the passage quoted from *Parsifal* and the excerpt from *Tristan* (see Appendix) contain successions of dominant seventh chords that may be said not to resolve at all. In both examples, chords that are clearly dominant sevenths in spelling and sound proceed to other dominant sevenths, but not in dominant relationship one to another. In the *Parsifal* quotation, the sevenths proceed directly, and by half steps (E, E♭, D, D♭, C); they slide, exactly as diminished sevenths often do. (See again the Chopin example.) In the *Tristan* excerpt, the dominant sevenths are at intervals of minor thirds (D♭|C♯–E–G) and are separated by intervening measures that may be construed in various ways, perhaps as dominant sevenths with diminished fifths, but that are in any case subordinate connecting links in the harmonic chain.

These "dominant sevenths" have nevertheless not lost all of their traditional association. They have, in a sense, lost all "regular" function, as understood in traditional practice; the sound of a recognizable and common harmonic note arrangement is present, and one can verify aurally and visually the notes and intervals (as, for example, G–B–D–F or E–G♯–B–D), yet these chords no longer even sound like dominants. We no longer expect them to resolve to immediately relevant tonic triads, but, on the other hand, we are not surprised if, on occasion, they do. In the context cited, the function of these sevenths is one of relative repose, and also one of extending tonal perspective. Of this, more will be said below.

These dominant sevenths are perhaps the most direct and simple clues to the understanding of the Wagnerian chromatic style, which is, notwithstanding Wagner's debts to his predecessors and contemporaries, one of the great original styles in the history of music. Wagner remains a "tonal" composer, and his harmony, despite its extension and its occasional diffuseness, is still traditional. Cadences in *Tristan* and *Parsifal* are still V–I, and are as strong and unequivocal as any in "classical" composers, when Wagner so intends them.* The dominant seventh, in other words, functions and resolves "regularly," or in terms of traditional convention, when the context requires it. All of the primary mechanisms of tonal harmony, as understood and applied by Bach,

* See Appendix, No. 20, *Parsifal*, end of Act II, as an example of a strong final cadence.

Mozart, and Beethoven, are also to be found in Wagner. What Wagner contributed to tradition was in part technical: a new texture based on the non-harmonic tone projected to great length and unprecedented emphasis, and the most extreme exploitation of harmonic ambiguities. But his most radical innovation was primarily esthetic; as we shall attempt to show, this was a new sense of musical time and therefore inevitably of musical form.

The sonata form, through Beethoven, depends on structural harmonic pivots or points of reference, often highly elaborated, but nevertheless always present. These are essentially the mechanisms of V–I harmony, extended yet recognizable. When these fundamental syntactical relations are blurred, as in Wagner, sonata form collapses. After Beethoven, the sonata form lost its force, and it is a little-disputed fact in musical history that the "romantic" 19th-century composers, until the arrival of Brahms, were not very successful in manipulating the sonata form. On formal grounds, they have always been criticized. Brahms solved the problem of the symphony and the sonata in a more or less traditional way, yet even Brahms suffers by comparison with Beethoven or the earlier masters of Classical style. It was only Wagner who perceived the problem clearly enough to solve it in a new way. Wagner, as noted in a previous chapter, understood that the problem was one of time-scale. His forms, although they retain many fundamental elements of organization on harmonic principles and traditional practice, are primarily melodic and contrapuntal. While Wagner retains the principle of key or tonality—every section of *Tristan* or *Parsifal* has a signature—this becomes in his musical design essentially the principle of the single key. It is almost impossible, therefore, to speak of modulation in Wagner. This is of course not true of his earlier works or even of all passages in his later ones, but it unquestionably holds for the most advanced, revolutionary, and characteristic passages in *Tristan* and *Parsifal*.

One of the first things that should be noticed in the passage of *Tristan* cited in the Appendix is that it has a key signature of three flats. The passage—nominally, at least—is in C minor. It is important to remember that Wagner invariably used key signatures, although they change frequently; the fact is an indication of a manner of thought with respect to tonal organization. There are, of course, simpler passages in Wagner, where key is relatively stable and obvious; in a passage such as the one with which we are concerned, however, it is something of a strain on ingenuity to relate all of it to the key of C. Allusion to a center of C is made in the last few bars, but the tonic triad is never heard, and indeed we do not, in this short passage, ever come to a point of rest. The essential point is that one cannot, from the standpoint of over-all structure or tonality, take a short passage from *Tristan* or *Parsifal* as material for fruitful study. The tonal units are so extended that an examination of detail in short excerpts risks the loss of the large outline. The excerpt we have chosen (from Act I, Scene II) shows certain technical usages worth studying; but to be fully understood it must be carried to its first real cadence, several score pages later, where the key signature changes to one flat. In a still larger but still real sense, the essential unit is not even the complete Scene, but the entire Act, which is centered on C. The same considerations hold for the excerpt from Act II of *Parsifal*. The entire Act is centered on the key of B minor, and the excerpt (centering on C) is related on the largest time-scale to the basic key as an extension of the Neapolitan sixth.

Examination of the passages from *Tristan* and *Parsifal*, inconclusive as they are from the larger standpoint of harmonic form and organization, nevertheless will demonstrate a number of characteristics of Wagner's idiom. One remarks at once the difficulty of naming or identifying every vertical combination, even when one has come to conclusions concerning non-harmonic tones. With these noted, one still is aware of the almost inexhaustible variety of vertical combinations that may be created through linear movement. Analysis, such as is attempted in the Appendix, shows that even in these short excerpts the "area" of the key has been immensely extended; if the passages are indeed centered around C, they include, within a brief enough time, harmonies such as dominant sevenths on F♯ that are relatively remote. And yet we can recognize tonally relevant elements none the less. It is questionable that anyone except a trained musician with an exceptional ear will hear the passages in the manner in which they can be visually analyzed. The analysis, despite this, has a value if it helps to demonstrate the continuing logic of traditional harmony at its extreme extension.

There is a temptation to consider "analysis" as a purely intellectual pastime or problem, and one must candidly concede that "analysis" may be used to prove a preconceived theory. When, in music, "analysis" succeeds in demonstrating something that cannot be heard, or justified as a logic of sound rather than of abstract conception, it is useless. For this reason, the possibilities of many alternate analyses should always be held open, and the student is asked to consider again the caution expressed in the Preface to this book. His goal should be to use such tools as are provided towards the understanding of music as it is heard and performed, by himself as the hearer or performer.

Specifically, it may indeed be possible to demonstrate analytically or theoretically that these passages from *Tristan* and *Parsifal* are in C. We have used the term "centered on C" as a more realistic approximation. One does not hear these passages, despite key signatures, as limited to C; on the contrary, they, and the larger works from which they are taken, may be said to prove the truth of Busoni's assertion about the *one* key of our tradition. Busoni's thought was that of a man of his time, the end of the Classical-Romantic harmonic tradition, and he is proved correct by Wagner and by the music of his time. The "area" of a key, in Wagner, has been so expanded as to include all keys, and, as has been suggested above, with this expansion the Classical forms are no longer possible. The technical dilemma posed by the great accomplishment of Wagner made it necessary for the 20th century to find new solutions or to attempt, as in neo-classicism, to revive older ones. Tonal harmony, as such, had reached its limit.

It is not less interesting to consider the esthetic implications of Wagnerian harmonic style. It is again necessary that the student hear or study a work of Wagner in its entirety, or at least in one of its larger constituent parts. What one cannot fail to notice, as a basic—and perhaps on the whole the most important—characteristic of the harmonic movement is its continuous motion, its avoidance or postponement of full or final cadences. This is, in Wagner, not so much a technical mannerism, and an expression of the unity of the keys themselves, as it is a symbol of movement towards infinite time. The traditional cadence is a boundary in time; the ideals of classical art include boundary, limitation, and proportion. Classical music evolves in finite time; the meaning of form in classical music is apportionment in fixed relation, and this is the formal significance of traditional harmonic structure. Romantic art, in general, seeks to go beyond limitations of time and space, and to suggest something without physical or psychological boundary. In this respect Wagner remains the great romantic artist. In his music, tonal harmonic perspective is carried as far as possible without destroying the principle of tonality itself. The inclusiveness of the tonal relations in Wagner eliminates proportioned division of motion and rest; it begins to destroy harmonically generated form by carrying it to a limit that succeeding generations of musicians recognized as such. The infinite movement of harmony, or its manipulation towards unbounded and unlimited motion, brought the end of development in the symbolic language of traditional harmony. The problem of music after Wagner was not one of consonance and dissonance, not one of "harmony" as such, but one of new principles for the rational and meaningful organization of sounds in a limited continuum of time.

Appendix

Appendix

The examples here given are chosen primarily because they are representative both of harmonic technical problems and of important harmonic styles. A subordinate consideration in choosing them was that most of them are not difficult to play, and can be managed by most students who have had a modest training at the piano. A few do not fall into this category, and these the student should try to hear, preferably in "live" performances by others, but failing that, in adequate recordings. If they are merely "analyzed," and not heard, there is no point in working with them.

Many of the examples are deliberately not "analyzed" in full. With the tools provided, the student may continue to study them and to draw analytical conclusions according to his own understanding.

No "analyses" are submitted as definitive. If the student has followed the text, he will understand that this is a central point in the author's thesis. Almost any piece of music, even a simple one, usually offers a number of interesting possibilities from the standpoint of construction or analytical discussion. It is good mental exercise, and good ear-training as well, if the student considers several alternatives as foundations for a logic of hearing.

In many instances, chords are indicated simply by their appropriate Roman numerals (as traditionally designated), without figures indicating inversions. It is expected that the student will recognize that a C-major triad with E as its lowest note is in first inversion and that he is prepared to regard it as such if any special harmonic situation is involved.

From a standpoint of thorough study, it would have been most advantageous to have been able to use nothing but complete compositions in every case, or at least, in some instances, very much longer excerpts. It is, however, quite obviously impractical to provide these in a book not designed as an anthology. But the author hopes that the student will, on his own, find and study not only the complete works from which these selections are taken, but also a number of other representative works. Unless he does so, he will be avoiding a major obligation of study and of learning, and will also be demanding of this book more than any single volume can properly promise.

1. J. S. BACH

Prelude in C major, *The Well-Tempered Clavier,* Book I

This key work has been mentioned and discussed at a number of points in the Introduction and text. It is, to repeat, a model of what C major, or key in general, means.

The harmonic proportion of the Prelude requires careful attention and study. The key of C is set forth clearly in all of its primary aspects, with attention directed to the dominant and the supertonic as the fundamental points of support. With respect to the subdominant, it will be noted that it does not in any instance proceed directly to the dominant; instead, it proceeds to II, which

in turn goes to V. The diminished seventh chords are all completely unequivocal, functioning as dominants in the most direct
connection. The diminished seventh in measure 28 (F♯–A–C–E♭)
is sometimes said to be misspelled, with E♭ written for D♯. In
either spelling, the movement of the chord is perfectly logical.
Measure 23 has also occasionally given rise to argument as to which
of the upper tones is non-harmonic (B or C). It seems clear
enough that the C is the non-harmonic tone, carried over or suspended from the previous measure, and resolving to B in the following. The harmony is thus a diminished seventh (B–D–F–A♭)
or VII⁷.

There is an eight-measure pedal on the dominant (measures
24–31) and a four-measure pedal on the tonic to conclude the
Prelude. The harmonies above these pedals are of course to be
regarded as independent of these pedal tones. Measure 33 is a typical example of the IV/II ambiguity; the D's at the conclusion of
the measure surely have enough force to be considered essential
harmonic notes, and we again have the case of IV as an incomplete
II, the understood root being in this instance actually supplied
before the movement to the dominant.

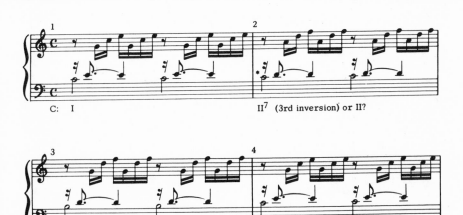

2. LEOPOLD MOZART

Polonaise, from *Notebook for* W. A. *Mozart,* 1762

There is little to add about this small piece. (See text, Chapters I, II, III.) The importance of the piece, a typical miniature of the 18th century, is that it sets out for the student a characteristic pattern of I–II–V–I, with a minimum of non-harmonic tones, and these of the simplest kind. But it illustrates also elementary principles of harmonic form. One should note that the dominant seventh is used sparingly (measures 4 and 10). The manner in which it is used also is suggestive; it does not carry through the measure.

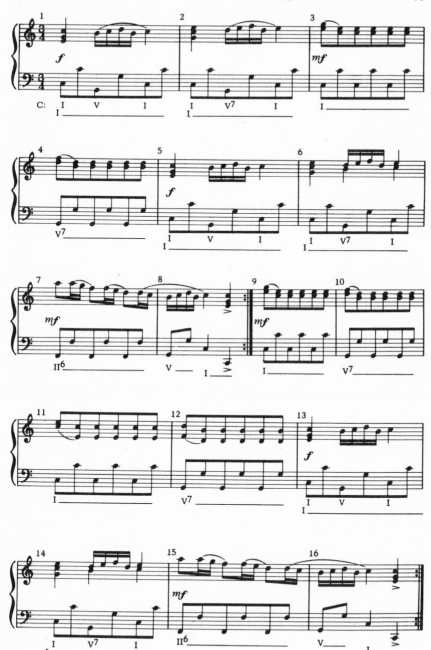

3. MUZIO CLEMENTI

Sonatina in G, Opus 36, No. 2

The first movement has been discussed in some detail in Chapter IX. The student should examine and study the second movement in an equally careful manner.

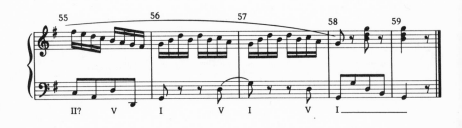

4. W. A. MOZART

"Viennese" Sonatina in A (1st movement)

As noted, this sonatina movement is rather more sophisticated than the Clementi, and covers a wider harmonic area. The sub-divisions, also, are more subtle and suggestive. The second measure offers a fine range of possibilities for the assiduous technician, and is an excellent illustration of a harmonic overlapping that contains elements of IV, II, and V simultaneously. The first two eighth notes (literally spelling a IV ♯ in the two voices) may even be construed as a I, by the same reasoning and aural convention that makes us accept the I ♯ as being usually an aspect of V.

The third measure offers another type of ambiguity. On the whole, it should probably be construed as suggesting V, the ascending scale in thirds being the most salient feature. But one may subdivide, and be conscious of the passing sounds of II, IV, I, and perhaps even VI. The student should consider thoughtfully how very greatly a different *phrasing* will alter the harmonic impression.

Suppose, for example, one were to slur the first eighth of the bar to the second, the third to the fourth, and so on. (Mozart's original phrasing is not established.) Tempo, of course, will also be a factor.

(Reference to the scale as a melodic suggestion of harmony has been made in Chapter VII, in connection with the first inversion series. A scale passage in thirds functions in the same manner.)

In measure 8, an uncertainty is not resolved until the third quarter. The A and C♯ may represent two notes of I (A–C♯–E) or two notes of VI (F♯–A–C♯). Here is a perfect example, in miniature, of the way in which an understanding of harmonic language demands that the ear travel back and forward in time. There are, *visually*, other possible constructions of the measure. If the G♯ in the lower voice is construed as anything more than a neighboring tone, a major seventh chord on I is suggested; in this case the second half of the measure, with the sound of the C♯ *dissociated*, might be heard as IV. Syntactical sense is evident both ways. How does the student hear it? To what extent is performance a factor? The student might attempt a fuller version of this measure (in context of course), adding notes that might make various possibilities explicit.

Exactly the same ambiguity occurs at the beginning of the development, the pattern of measures 8 and 9 being repeated identically at a different pitch level. We cannot be sure of the significance of the G♮–E until the second half of the bar brings us the C♮. Nor can we be sure of the syntactical value of the C–E–G triad until we have the F♯ triad resolving to B. It is then, in a retrospective flash of perception, that we understand the beautifully simple mechanism of the N⁶–V–I (on B or II). Note also how the II is confirmed in the following two measures, and what satisfaction the ear then takes in the repetition of the pattern (a perfect sequence of course on II–I) on A.

Returning for a moment, one should note carefully the ending of the exposition. The question of modulation has been discussed in connection with the Clementi Sonatina; the same considerations, in general, may be applied here. It is possible that the

Mozart more clearly does not modulate, and that one has a more definite impression of closing on the dominant of the original key. The distinction is largely verbal. The complex V of the last two-and-one-half measures includes references to the original I (A major), which perhaps may be heard as IV of a new key or center (E major), but which may also (since the E in the bass is a pedal point) be construed as standing for II or II⁷ of E. Again, one should not propose a hard and fast analytical construction, but study carefully the weight and quality of the harmonic subdivisions, and consider the possibilities. Whatever analytical construction is made, the ear accepts the movement to the E-major triad as quite firm and satisfying, and that, from the aural standpoint, is all that is required.

After the sequence II–(V)–I at the beginning of the exposition, a further harmonic expansion is presented through the mechanism of the circle of fourths, with a repeated VI–II–V–I in quarter notes, and a final confirmation of tonality through a II–V–I in greater length. We see here again, on a small scale, an essential feature of sonata-form developments: the elaboration of harmonic scope or area, and the orderly return to the home key. The recapitulation presents nothing new until measure 22, where the original ascending scale in thirds becomes an ascending scale in sixths, even more clearly suggesting a first inversion series, but preserving the same suggestions as before of triads of I, II, V, IV, and perhaps VI. In measure 33, what became clear as VI in the exposition becomes II or IV (it is incomplete), going to V and thence to I. The final two-and-one-half measures are an exact repetition (on A) of the ending of the exposition, and in their internal construction pose exactly the same questions. This time, however, one knows that it is a final cadence, and that A can be nothing other than the tonic. The reason for the difference in the way the two cadences (exposition and recapitulation) are heard is simply that in the latter case *all* the movement, from the very beginning of the development, has been directed back at A.

5. C. M. VON WEBER
Wiegenlied, Opus 13, No. 2

This interesting 16-measure song provides a clear example of the IV chord as what Tovey suggested be called the "anti-dominant." The IV chord here is a balance, on the other side of I from V; it does not push the ear towards a final cadence, but rather halts it momentarily, and is a "brake" on forward motion.

The phrase structure of the piece is worth careful study. Note the I–I–V–I construction of the opening phrase, as contrasted with the extended movement of the second four measures ending on V. For a piece of this size, the harmonic "area," extending as far as V⁷ of III, is noteworthy; it is controlled with admirable skill. To be noted also is the fact that there are, in the space of a few short measures, pure dominant sevenths on G, B, D, and C.

6. W. A. MOZART

Adagio, from *Adagio and Allegro*
for a Musical Clockwork, K. 594 *

This work is discussed in the text, particularly in Chapter X.

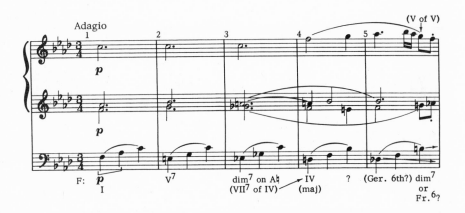

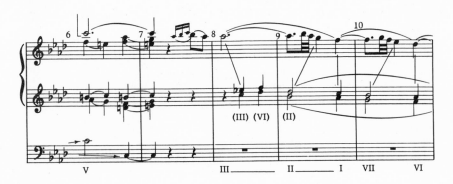

* This work is given, as is common, in organ score. There is also a version, by Mozart, for piano, four-hands.

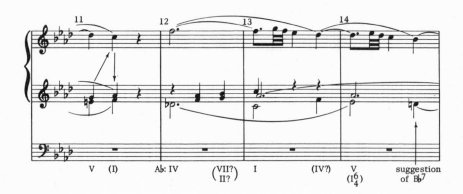

V   (I)   Ab: IV $\left(\begin{array}{c}\text{VII?}\\ \text{II?}\end{array}\right)$ I   (IV?)   V   suggestion
$\left(\text{I}^{6}_{4}\right)$ of Bb^7

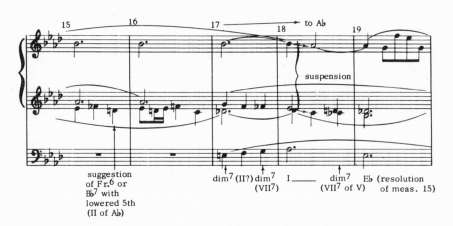

suggestion   dim^7 (II?) dim^7 I_____   dim^7 Eb (resolution
of Fr.^{6} or   (VII^7)   (VII^7 of V)   of meas. 15)
Bb^7 with
lowered 5th
(II of Ab)

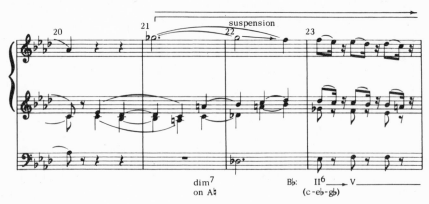

dim^7 Bb: II^6 ___→ V _____
on Ab   (c -eb-gb)

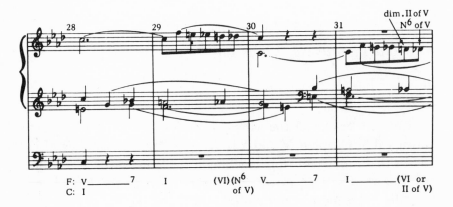

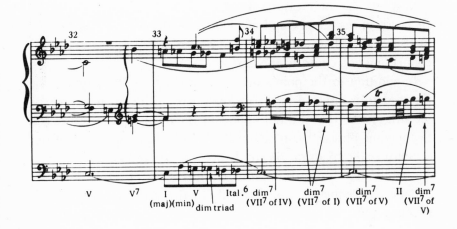

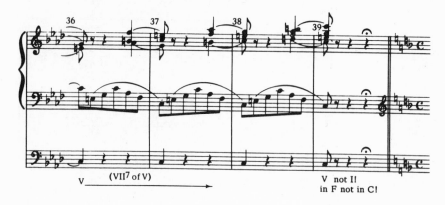

7. FRANZ SCHUBERT

Moment musical, Opus 94, No. 1 (opening page)

This first section of the *Moment musical* in C major has been discussed in Chapters V and VII. We have here a handling of C major that is different from anything to be found in Bach, Haydn, or Mozart. The long extensions of the sound of the I triad (especially measures 1–3 and 21–25) make possible the playful ambiguity (III/I) of measures 18–20, and the leaping away to the B♭ triads in measures 5 and 26. This is, as the student must see, a matter of total harmonic sense and design, not simply a matter of connecting one chord to the next.

In addition to the points discussed in the text, the attention of the student is directed to the introduction, in the last measures, of seventh chords that did not appear in the opening 8 measures. In the opening phrase, the triads on B♭, E♭, and D are repeated; at the conclusion the triads on B♭ and D become B♭⁷ and D⁷ respectively. An additional forward impulse is thus given to this typically Schubertian sequence, and the final cadence becomes all the more effective.

8. FRANZ SCHUBERT

Impromptu, Opus 142, No. 3
(Theme and closing section)

This Impromptu is a Theme and Variations which the student may study with profit in its entirety. The Variations are essentially melodic variations on a harmony that does not change greatly in its essentials, but introduces considerable variety in detail.

The chordal analysis presents no problems. The theme is simple, and the first period or section goes no further than I, II, and V. But the second period begins at once with a major III (V of VI) repre-

senting a relatively great distance from which to work back to the
tonic; this movement, also a favorite of Mozart and Beethoven,
here has a particularly fresh and delightful sound. The logical forward connection of the return to the tonic is readily apparent. In
measure 14, we have the first appearance of IV, here, as so often
in traditional practice, with very evident suggestions of the II.

The conclusion of the Impromptu (Coda), with its echo of the
theme, is an interesting example both of harmonic "interpolation"
and of textural change. In measure 122, the student will note that
between I and II (original theme) there is now a V^7 of II, and
that what was originally a II^7 going to V is now a simple II without
the seventh. Here again, as with the statement of the theme, the
student will note the repetition of the cadence. This is not a
mannerism; it is necessitated by the time-scale of the work.

III (V of VI)   VI ————————   II (V of V)   V   VI⁷

II (V of V)   V———7   I   I (V⁷ of IV)   IV   dim⁷
                                (with suggestions   (VII⁷ of V)
                                    of II)   dominant
                                                   root (c)

II (V⁷of V) V———————7 I   note second
    (I⁶₄)   (V)   ending!

B♭:   I   V⁷   V⁷   I   VI   II
                                 (appogg. VII⁷ᵇI)

9. ROBERT SCHUMANN

Valse noble, from *Carnaval*, Opus 9

A piece obviously in B♭, but commencing with a diminished seventh (VII⁷) which eases, as is so often the case, into a dominant seventh (V⁷). The interest here is partly the emphasis given this movement by placing the important "sliding" voice in the bass. One is almost tempted to describe the G♭ as nothing more (or less) than an appoggiatura to the F. However we wish to describe this, we have three measures of active dominant harmony before the tonic appears, made more effective by the strong appoggiatura on C. In measure 6, the IV/II ambiguity is nicely illustrated. Is the harmony II⁷, or is the C an accented passing tone or appoggiatura? *

* In considering harmony in 19th-century piano music, it should be remembered that the sustaining pedal was available, and utilized.

The second section begins with the same relation just noted in the Schubert Impromptu (B♭ tonic immediately to III), in this case also a major triad, but with the seventh added, so that it is V⁷ of VI. It begins a sequence: V⁷ of VI–VI; V⁷ of II–II; and again V⁷ of VI–VI. Is there a modulation to G? What follows is fairly obvious: the composer takes one further step away, to V⁷ of III (in B♭), and brings this back to the III (again V⁷ of VI) with which the eight-measure phrase began. There is at this point a more or less "fluid" break (a point to watch in performance, it may be mentioned) and a repetition of the phrase. The sixteen measures (eight measures repeated) are probably most clearly heard (and analyzed) as an exploration or exploitation of the area of VI, as part of the original key, rather than as even a "passing" modulation to G.

Measures 24–25 should be studied carefully. The F♯ of the dominant seventh on D (V⁷ of VI) becomes G♭, enharmonically, and the D moves by half step to E♭, the C and the A remaining. This simple movement transforms a dominant seventh on D to a diminished seventh on A (A–C–E♭–G♭), to which an F is added,* firmly in the bass, to establish a strong dominant of B♭, the point of departure. This mechanism is a most important one; it is one of the pivots most often used in music from Beethoven to Brahms. With measure 24, we have by a magnificently simple step returned to the opening of the piece.

The final eight measures convert the opening phrase into a conclusion. Note the change of the G to A♭ in measure 36, making a non-harmonic tone into one that suggests fleetingly V⁷ of IV, and the beautiful and satisfying *minor* IV that follows. The next-to-last measure now is unequivocally II⁷ (V⁷ of V), and the final cadence is strong and unmistakable.

---

* Cf. Bach, Chapter X, F to D.

10. ROBERT SCHUMANN

Song, *Ich kann's nicht fassen, nicht glauben*, from *Frauenliebe und -leben*, Opus 42

This is a typical example of Schumann's harmonic style, especially in its use of various seventh chords, including dominant seventh with augmented fifth and dominant seventh with diminished fifth. The latter, as noted in the text, is hard to distinguish from the augmented six-four-three, or "French sixth," but the question of nomenclature is scarcely one of vital importance. As these chords occur in this piece, the interval of the augmented sixth, although not in the outer voices, resolves outward to the dominant octave, but it would do the same as part of a V^7 of V.

Modulation is certainly a theoretically present question in this work. For approximately 12 measures in the middle, there is a strong suggestion of change to E♭ major. Nevertheless, one is never very far from the original C.

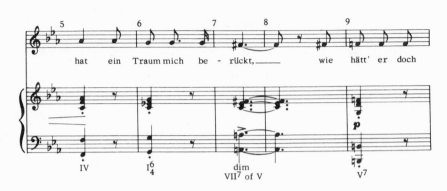

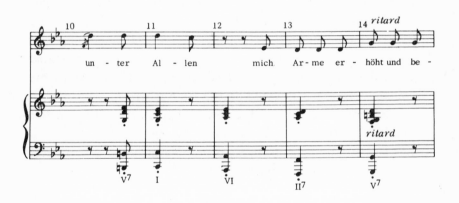

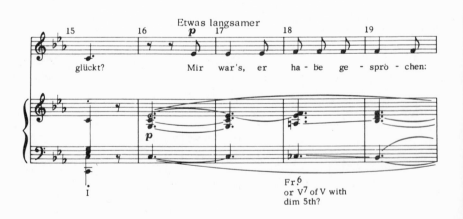

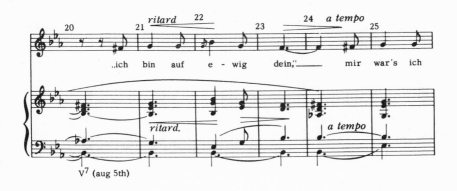

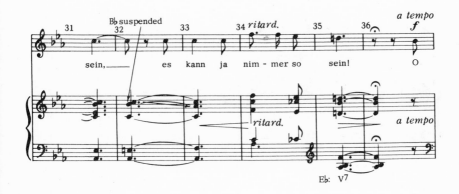

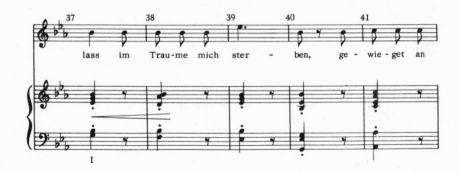

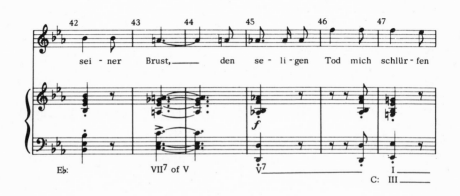

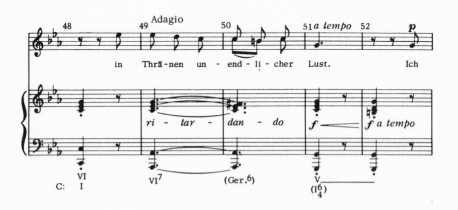

kann's nicht fas - sen, nicht glau - ben, es hat ein

Traum mich be - rückt,____ wie hätt er doch un - ter Al - len

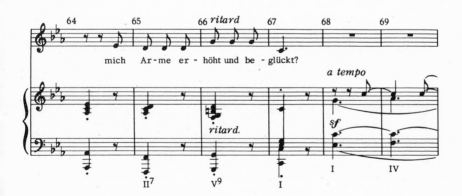

mich Ar - me er - höht und be - glückt?

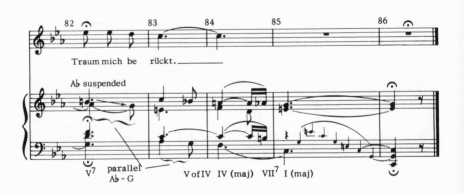

Chorale and Chorale Preludes on
Liebster Jesu, wir sind hier

The purpose of juxtaposing several of Bach's settings of the same chorale melody will be apparent. The student should begin by carefully studying the simplest version (a), and proceed through the others, noting variations in harmony and all other features, such as melodic variation and elaboration and other techniques of expansion.

The ambitious student may take similar groups of settings by Bach (for example, a half-dozen or more versions of *Allein Gott in der Höh' sei Ehr'*) and make a comparative study of the same type.

12. L. VAN BEETHOVEN
Piano Concerto No. 3 (opening of 2nd movement)

See brief discussion in Chapter VII. In addition to the resolutions of V^7 to VI, and the handling of the third relation, the student should note the harmonic movement of measures 9–12 with particular attention. The "unprepared" movement to the G-major triad in measure 9 introduces a wonderfully subtle and interconnected pattern of movement back to E. The dominant sevenths on D and B both resolve upward by step (to E and C♮); the basses on the downbeats outline the triad C♮–E–G♮ (C-major triad), which is heard explicitly in measure 11, and which reveals itself as VI (lowered, or N of V). The A♯ at the end of the measure prepares the diminished-seventh appoggiatura to V, making the cadence in measure 12.

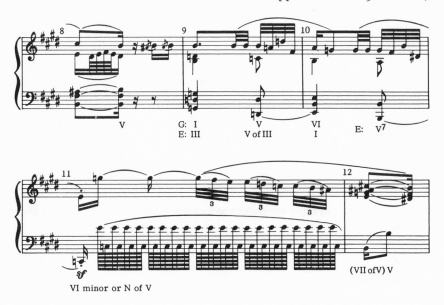

13. JOHANNES BRAHMS

Intermezzo in B♭, Opus 76, No. 4

This familiar piece has much of interest from a harmonic view-point. Most notably, the student will observe that although it is in B♭, the tonic triad is not actually heard until measure 44, and is not unequivocally established as such until measure 46. The insistence on the V[7] and the exploitation of the minor IV show clearly how areas of a key other than the tonic may be emphasized even in a relatively short piece. This type of manipulation is characteristic of Brahms, as are the many embellishing non-harmonic tones applied to fairly simple progressions, and also to harmonically static passages. Suggestions of other harmonies occur constantly, and the question of harmonic division and subdivision is sometimes difficult to resolve. Yet the piece is considerably simpler in harmonic plan than may appear at first sight or hearing.

The opening measures may be construed as an extended V⁷. At (1), the B♮ and G♯ are accented non-harmonic tones moving to C and A. The sound momentarily produced is interesting: it is the same "half-diminished" seventh sound (F–A♭–C♭–E♭) that we have noticed in Chopin and Wagner (see Chapter X). But it is obviously not the same in function here, except as it remotely resembles the appoggiatura to a V⁷ in *Parsifal*. The G♯ is transformed to A♭, with the continuation of the pattern, in measure 7, and in measure 8 we hear an A♭–major triad (first inversion), continuing through measures 9 and 10. Here is another example of the manner in which we understand heard harmonies retrospectively; we cannot be certain that this is N⁶ in G until we have reached G, via a diminished seventh on F♯ and a dominant seventh on D, in measure 14. We have an extended II–V–I, a real modulation to G, beginning with the eighth measure.

Measures 14–20 constitute a confirmation of G as a center, with references to IV and suggestions of V of IV, as the only harmonies other than I. But the I chord is embellished in thirds and sixths from above and below, and the augmented sixth interval, first heard in measure 12 (E♭–C♯) is again used to give emphasis to the dominant octave D of the new key center.

The half-measure ending the section is a minor IV of the original key of B♭, and leads back to the opening rather surprisingly, but effectively. As a continuation to the second section the E♭–minor triad continues, with its minor third, G♭ (which is, of course, its most striking element), becoming the foundation of an extended passage. A dominant seventh on G♭, suggesting the tonic of C♭, is heard for seven measures, eventually resolving "deceptively" in measure 30 to a seventh chord on A♭. In measure 31, a diminished seventh on G♮, becoming a dominant seventh on E♭ by the half-step change of F♭ to E♭, confirms a resolution to A♭ in measure 32. Thence through the minor IV and V⁷ of B♭, a return to the opening key and figuration of the piece is effected. Of particular interest here are measures 40 through 45, in which the V⁷ of B♭ is avoided. The A♭ triad in measure 40 proves in this instance not to function as it did originally, as N⁶ of G, but rather as a IV of IV (A♭ to E♭), serving as preparation, in a sense, for the final cadence, a splendid and effective example of the minor IV used to precede the final I. Note also the suggestion of the chord of the doubly augmented fourth (G♭–B–C♯–E♮) beginning with measure 46. In a real sense, this chord, with its strong drive to the dominant octave (F–F), is the replacement for the dominant.

The piece as a whole is of the utmost harmonic sophistication, yet it is far from complex. It dwells on certain "areas" of its key of B♭, notably that of VI (G), IV minor (E♭), and lowered or Neapolitan II (C♭). These of course are in root relations of thirds one to another, and, like all harmonies with roots a third apart, these overlap. It is the overlapping relationship of triads represented by C♭–E♭–G♭ (G♮)–B♭ (and D/D♭) that is manipulated so charmingly and effectively throughout the piece. Again, it will be noted that in the second section of the piece, the triad on C♭ is, like the tonic B♭ triad in the first section, not actually heard; it is known to be present, in a manner of speaking, through the constant presence of its dominant seventh. The second section repeats the pattern of the first: the dominant seventh, after all, does not resolve as V⁷ to I, but in both cases as V⁷ to VI (F–seventh to G; G♭–seventh to A♭).

Intermezzo in B♭ minor, Opus 116, No. 2
(beginning)

This Intermezzo, like the one preceding, appears at first sight to be more complex harmonically than is actually the case. The opening may be construed in several ways. Most obviously it involves two first-inversion triads (II and I). We have here, however, an interesting use of the minor II (a diminished triad) in such a way as to suggest that it represents an incomplete diminished seventh on the leading-tone, or by extension, an incomplete dominant ninth. This suggestion should not be taken literally; the II here simply suggests such a dominant derivation, but the suggestion is given added force by the interesting extension it receives in measures 9 and 10. (See schematization.) The dominant seventh (V^7) on F in measure 8 resolves in measure 9 to a minor triad on G♭. (The spelling should properly be G♭–B♭♭–D♭.) In measure 10 the addition of the E♭ in the bass gives one of those marvelously useful ambiguities that the master composers used so effectively. The ear re-orients quickly, from the impression of a "half-diminished" seventh on E♭ (E♭–G♭–B♭♭–D♭), to that of a diminished seventh on A♮ (enharmonic B♭♭) with the D♭ suspended and destined to move to C. This is syntactically what does happen. With the A♮ dropped out, as the D♭ moves to C, we are left with the exact harmony that we heard at the opening of the piece.

For the rest, the student will observe that the progression of the first section of the Intermezzo is a simple circle of fourths.

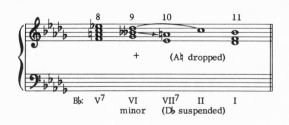

15. FRANZ LISZT

Tarantella, from *Années de Pèlerinage, Venezia e Napoli* (concluding page)

This page is given as an example of late Romantic use of "disjunct" (i.e. syntactically unconnected) triads in a strongly tonal context. Note that the series of these triads is preceded and followed by strongly emphasized V–I in the key (G). The series, really sequences of a sort, of simple chords a fourth apart (B–E, G–C, E♭–A♭, D–G), is actually not out of the key at all, although its relevance is not obvious when it is heard at tempo. But the spacing-out of the last four chords clarifies their functions perfectly, and the last twelve measures simply hammer home the tonic, with one effective stop on the minor IV.

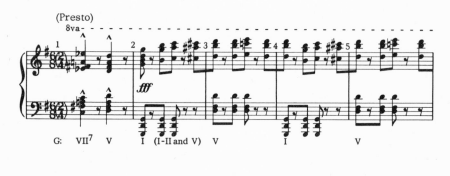

16. FRÉDÉRIC CHOPIN
Passage from Mazurka in C minor, Opus 56, No. 3

This passage has been discussed in Chapter X. The harmonic reduction appended here may help clarify the essential movement, but it should be emphasized that several constructions are possible. It will be evident that an analysis by attempting to find names for all the chords is useless. What is important is to try to find the connections.

An example of the difficulty may be found in measure 11 of the passage, where the spelling (B♭–D---A♭) surely suggests a dominant seventh (F missing) on B♭. But the three notes in no way move in this sense. The B♭ and A♭ both proceed to A♮s, suggesting that the A♭ should properly be spelled G♯, and giving us a simple (Italian) augmented sixth chord with an obvious resolution. (The C♯ is clearly an accented neighboring tone.) We are at this point no longer firmly oriented to C as a tonic, and even the suggestion of a momentary clarification on E♭ is too transient to indicate a new point of reference. The passage from measure 7 until the N⁶–V–I cadence in measures 16–17–18 is one in which tonality is temporarily suspended. Note that these 9 measures contain five diminished seventh chords, one augmented sixth, and one measure (9) that is highly ambiguous and difficult even to classify in terms of essential chordal structure.

The student should examine this Mazurka in its entirety, and find similar passages in other works of Chopin.

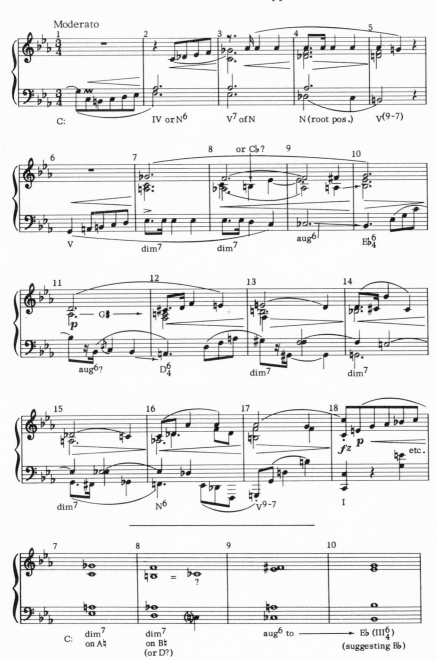

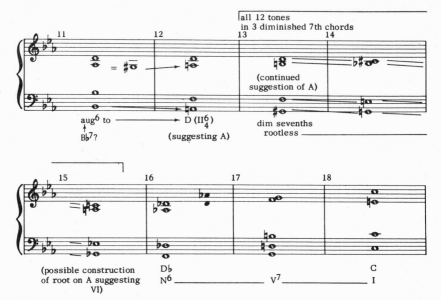

Note chromatic main progression of passage: roots Eb - D - Db - C
                                             bar   10 -12- 16 - 18

17. FRÉDÉRIC CHOPIN
Nocturne in C minor, Opus 48, No. 1
(concluding pages)

Note: The tempo of the concluding section is given as *doppio movimento* (twice as fast), following an original tempo indication of Lento. The student should if possible hear, perform, or study the entire piece.

The chordal indications given with this passage are for roots only. The interesting material for study is the occurrence of chords of the ninth, eleventh, and thirteenth on these roots. There can be no question that these chords are heard, and meant to be heard.

Yet one will note that each of them resolves into a seventh, or includes some type of non-harmonic tone that resolves without much delay. But the texture is continuously rich, and the passage is a magnificent example of exploitation of piano sonority. The cadence has been discussed in Chapter VI.

The basic harmonic progression of the passage, with all its vertical elaboration, is that of the circle of fourths. In most of his music, Chopin remains essentially a classicist, and many of his most ornamented passages prove to be harmonically as simple and direct as this.

18. RICHARD WAGNER

Tristan und Isolde (excerpt from Act I, Scene 2)

This passage will be found near the beginning of the scene, and should be compared directly with the opening measures of the familiar Prelude. If possible, the student should also examine the remainder of the first part of this scene, up to the change of key to one flat (page 17, Breitkopf & Härtel vocal score). Orchestral score should be used if possible; the piano reduction is generally adequate with respect to harmonic movement, but much detail is lost.

The student will note first that the vocal line includes a complete ascending chromatic scale, twelve notes, D to D, divided into four equal and symmetrical phrases, each compassing a minor third. Beginning with the fourth measure of this excerpt, the parallel with the opening of the Prelude is exact as to pitch and harmonic progression. The two halves of the opening motif are, however, overlapped in this passage.

One striking difference in the two passages will be observed: the key signatures are different, although, as noted above, the pitch and harmonic progressions are identical through six measures. The Prelude opens in what is usually construed as A minor (with the appropriate signature) and the concert version ends clearly in A major. The passage cited here is ostensibly in C minor, changing to C major.

The conclusion to be drawn has been suggested in Chapter X. Tonality in Wagner is a matter of broad areas and lengthy evolution in time. Key is indicated clearly only at certain pivotal points, through conventional cadences and organization of related harmonies. The intervening passages are often in no identifiable key except, as previously suggested, in the single key that represents the ultimate extension of the "area" of any key. The last four measures of the passage given here indicate a gravitation towards C as a terminus, but it should be noted that after the change of key signature (to C major) another dominant seventh (on E) immediately moves into another region. (A minor is momentarily suggested, but C major is eventually reached.)

The symmetry of organization in this passage is evident on examination. The twelve-note chromatic scale is divided into four minor thirds, melodically and harmonically. Dominant seventh chords, with roots a minor third apart, are found in measures 4 (on Db/C♯), 6 (on E), and 8 (on G). These measures are preceded by harmonies that are difficult to define; they have the sounds of dominant sevenths with diminished fifths (as B–D♯–F–A or D–F♯–Ab–C) or of chords with augmented sixths. The lack of a tonal point of reference, however, makes all conventional considerations of this sort meaningless. Without a point of reference it is impossible to anticipate a resolution; once the pattern of the sequence has been established, one begins to anticipate continued motion without resolution. The reversal of the usual, or the suspension of anything resembling cadence, gives the "deceptive" resolution of the dominant seventh on G (measure 8) to the A♭ triad (measure 9) an unusual degree of force. Note that the crescendo (*pp* in measure 1 to *ff* in measure 9) is an essential part of this design.

From the viewpoint of "detached" analysis, one might identify the A♭ triad as VI of C minor, or N⁶ of V, but at its point of occurrence one can hardly be certain of this. The A major of measures 11 and 12 is a startling departure; it is structurally explicable in terms of the continued reference to the minor third: note that the melody, with its wide skips, is still E♭–C–A, all minor third intervals. Reference to C is once again clear with the IV minor in measure 13, and the two measures of dominant seventh on G (measures 15–16). The harmony in measure 14 leads to the dominant seventh on G; it may be construed as a V⁷ of V, with diminished fifth (D–F♯–A♭–C) or possibly as an augmented six-four-three (French sixth). Also to be noted is the exact parallelism between measures 7–8 and 14–15; the repetition of this harmonic pattern may be regarded as lending some support to the assumption of C as the understood tonal center.

The question of non-harmonic tones is not always an easy one to resolve in typical Wagnerian passages of this sort. In general, the pattern involves accents on tones that are non-harmonic, as is clearly the case with the first notes of the upper voice in measures 6 and 8 and elsewhere. But at the tempo indicated it is quite possible to hear almost every one of these tones as forming part of another rapidly changing, and elusive, harmonic configuration. Again, except in those cases involving a clearly defined and structurally significant harmonic sound, the categorizing of tones as harmonic or non-harmonic is largely an academic exercise. The essential of the idiom is constant motion, to which all tones contribute. The traditional mechanisms, of focusing the motion towards a point, are clear enough whenever they occur. The balance between the two is the essential secret of Wagner's art.

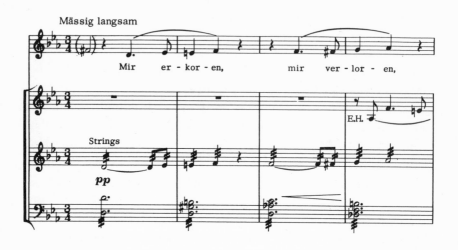

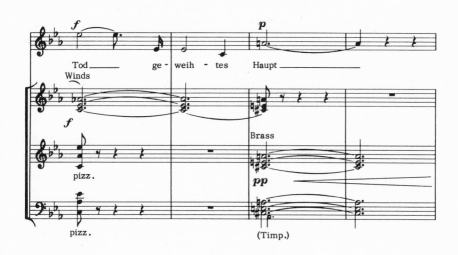

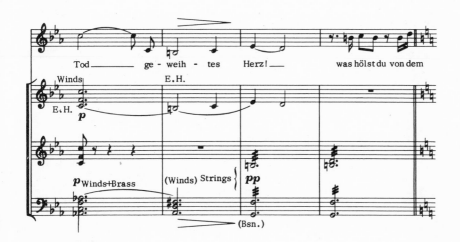

19. RICHARD WAGNER
Parsifal (excerpt from Act II)

Many of the generalizations made in connection with the preceding example are also applicable here. In general, this passage
defies conventional analysis by chord description, yet again it man-
ages to suggest a key orientation by occasional pivotal points that
are syntactically unequivocal. In the *con moto* passage, there are
repetitive patterns involving "normal" resolutions of dominant
seventh chords, and, as noted in Chapter X, these dominant
sevenths are preceded by "half-diminished" sevenths moving chromatically. Many other features of the passage have been discussed
as well in Chapter X.

The student should devote considerable time to a detailed study
of the passage. Again, reference to the orchestral score is highly
advisable.

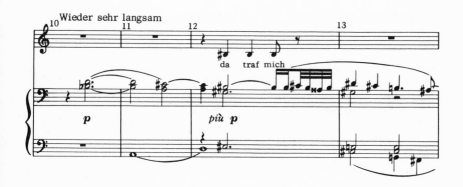

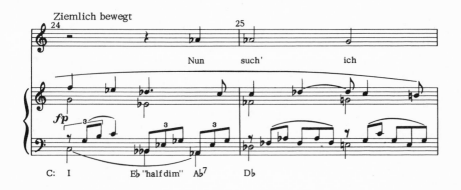

20. RICHARD WAGNER

Parsifal (end of Act II)

Act II of *Parsifal* ends, as it begins, in B minor. The concluding ten measures are a wonderfully extended V–I. The harmony of the climactic dominant (*ff*) is in effect a chord of the eleventh, which melts down, so to speak, with the diminution in intensity and volume, to a simple dominant seventh. The intervening harmonic sounds are all to be construed as passing; the emphasis is melodic, as an examination of the orchestral score will show. The stress is on the melodic movement (trumpet, violas, cellos) from the E♯ chromatically upward to the B, six measures from the end.

The central point here is that this cadence, however extended or embellished, is a perfectly conventional one, and it is on a scale that more than satisfies one's demand for finality.

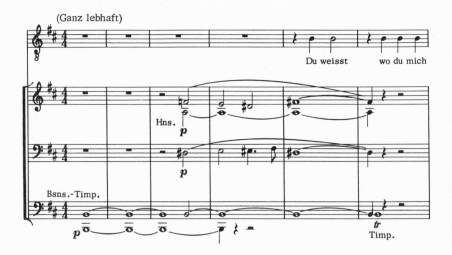

Index

Note: For terms such as tonic, dominant, triad, etc., which recur continually throughout the text, only those references have been included that apply to extensive explanatory passages.